Professional Western Training

Ranch **Pleasure**
Reining **Roping**

by gordon peacock

Dr. G.I.W. Cottam

This book is dedicated to my good friend Dr. G.I.W. Cottam who first suggested I write it.

Printed by
North Plains Press
Box 1950
Aberdeen, S.D. 57401

Contents

Introduction 6

1. Approach to Basics in Western Training 9

2. Communicating with Your Horse 12

3. Haltering and Leading the Colt 17

4. Riding and Training Equipment 26

5. Lunging the Horse 41

6. Preliminaries Prior to Riding 47

7. Starting the Green Colt 53

8. First Rides on Greenie 65

9. Further Lessons for Greenie 77

10. Figure Eight's, Beginning of Neckreining,
    and Backing Up 83

11. Loping and Further Reining 93

12. Collection, Leads, and Cues 101

13. Transition from Hackamore to Snaffle Bit 111

14. Finishing the Pleasure Horse 125

15. Starting the Reining Horse 133

16. Flying Change of Leads 139

17. Pivots 145

18. Roll Backs 152

19. Stops 159

20. Rope Horse Phase I 167

21. Rope Horse Phase II 174

22. Rope Horse Phase III 182

23. The Rearing Horse 191

24. Barrel Horse 196

25. Trailer Schooling 200

Conclusion 205

Introduction

I have been horseback on some kind of horse off and on ever since I was about six years old. My father was a farmer and although he kept about twenty head of horses around for the purpose of working them in the fields, he was not particularly interested in their ability as to riding qualifications.

Being a poor man, he could not, by choice, have the kind of work horses such as the better bred Percherons, Clydes-dales or Belgians. He had to settle for any kind of horse that could be broke and put in harness to do the field work. This led to his having quite a variety as to size. There were some that would weigh fourteen hundred pounds. Then there would be some that were a thousand to eleven-fifty pound weight and came off an Indian Reservation. These horses were about the right size for riding horses. Although their heritage was questionable, it being in the early 1920's, you could believe they were from a wild horse strain of blood. Anyway, these were my first horses that I had any experience with in my early riding career.

These Indian horses taught me a lot. They were branded and came from range country. They were also on the broncy side. I fooled with these horses as a kid and rode them to school. I herded cattle on them, and they also served as my transportation to any get-together or entertainment that was in the area. This covered a period of time until I had graduated from the eighth grade, which was the extent of my formal schooling.

Early in my youth I had an intense interest in teaching horses. I was always experimenting to teach one something new or different. The two horses I rode the most were trained to lie down or count their age with a front foot by pawing so many times. They would also nod up or down for a signal of yes or a shake of the head meaning no. I was real proud of their performance.

Horses were being used for farming and ranch operations at this time instead of tractors. Persons that were adept at harnessing, driving, and handling harness horses were quite numerous. I did my share of it.

I also got to observe the kind of bits used on these horses. The favorite and most widely used bit was what I would refer to now as the ring snaffle. They were made out of iron and steel. They were not any different than some on the market today basically with the exception of the width. They were wider to accommodate the wider, larger mouths of the heavier draft horses. They also made the narrower type for the buggy or smaller type horses.

I learned in my driving of these horses, that those horses kept in the bit under constant pressure on a long set of lines always seemed to pull a little stronger, as time went on, against the hands holding the reins. While horses that were given a little slack would hold and maintain the desired gait by the driver.

I think there's a point to be made here. If a horse under saddle is rode into the bit and kept there too steady in the riding, he will push into the bit a little more as time passes as he is being ridden. Care has to be exercised that the right amount of slack be used on the horse's mouth to keep him light and responsive. More people should be informed and educated about this particular part of horse handling in this day and age than is being done. When horses were being used from necessity there were enough informed horsemen to enlighten the less knowledgeable people. This led to most everybody having some general knowledge about it. When horses started to disappear from the scene so did the interest in passing on any experiences or knowledge about horses. A big gap resulted in horse savvy by the people in general. The old-timers with the knowledge died off or became inactive and the interest in horses was so slight that no one taught the younger people how to handle horses. Today's demand for horse knowledge is widespread.

I did not really get into training until about 1934. At this time the depression and drought were in full swing in most of the west. I found that I could usually get some horses to break when other work was almost impossible to obtain. After I became aware of this, I started to look more for this kind of work than any other. The more I did of it the more I liked it, and my interest in it increased.

As I pretty much covered both the southwest and northwest, I would run into about every kind of range horse there was to break and start. I would also on occasion be hired as a helper to a professional horse trainer. Some of these men were experts in this field. Some were hackamore men and excelled at it from its first use to turning out a finished spade-bit horse. I think that these men advising me helped me a lot. I also had the privilege of getting enough stock to practice on.

The broncs made me learn to ride. They also made me figure out where all the advantages were. It made me study every move they made while I was working around them on the ground. It was, I think, self-preservation that made me build a relationship with them and also how to communicate with them.

I married while in the service during World War II. After my discharge I tried farming for several years. I kept a couple of horses around but didn't really get back on any horses for pay until I had become discouraged with farming. We sold out and quit. The next fifteen years I devoted strictly to training horses. This was my sole occupation. I had no other job for a livelihood. My wife taught school, and I rode a lot of horses.

I wish to take this opportunity to thank all the people who brought me their stock to work. I owe them, because they kept me in business. I wish especially at this time to thank a retired M.D. by the name of Dr. G. I. W. Cottam, who was the one who first suggested I write this book. He was the owner of two mighty good horses that I had the privilege of putting some work on. Doc, as I called him, was a good friend and believe it or not, this man at almost eighty years old still sets a good saddle. He rides well and has owned some mighty good horses. Horseback riding has been a part of his life for many, many years.

 **1**

Approach to Basics in Western Training

The approach to basics in training horses is very important. There are certain fundamentals if learned and followed, are going to make training less complicated and will have a definite effect on the general job done on the horse throughout his training period.

There will never be a perfect horse either in conformation or his ability to perform. We strive at perfection and in the process of getting close a lot of work, time, and patience will be involved.

Let me give a description as to the ability or powers of the horse's mind to absorb what he learns. In my opinion a horse's mind can only absorb one act or one thing at a time. I think people should bear this in mind. For an example, I would work with a horse on one particular part of his training one step at a time. Whatever the subject I were trying to teach him, I would work slowly in the process. I would not try to work more than one subject at a time in the same training session, until I was sure the horse had a pretty good idea of what I was trying to teach him. Then when I knew that he had made some progress towards that particular part of his training, I would start another one. I would go back to the original subject every training period to refresh his memory and to improve on it. If you start too many new subjects all at one time, it will confuse the horse and lessen his chances to learn any of them well. If the horse is doing a subject of training fairly well and will repeat it pretty much the same in his efforts to do it, he's ready for a new subject. If it's over-done by confusing him with more than he can understand, he will tire of it and won't try as hard and will make more mistakes in doing any of them well.

One other thing might be said here, and it is very important, "patience." You cannot expect the horse to learn something new in a matter of minutes. You will be tested many times, but keep showing him what you want him to do. He will eventually grasp it.

Voice as an aid to training cannot be underestimated. You would probably use it a lot more in his early training, and what training you do on the ground with the horse, more so than you would after actual riding lessons start. However, in all likelihood, it will prove valuable throughout the horse's entire training, and to some extent throughout his entire life. Voice is one of the major factors in communication with the horse. It can be administered at the same time your hands are busy. It can be used at a distance without interfering with the training maneuvers. Voice can be used to reward a horse, can be used to discipline him, and to warn or caution him. It is fast. It can catch the horse in a mistake. It is quicker than the hand. This is one of the more significant parts in the area of communication.

Now let us get into some basic on how to use voice. I like to use it to get and keep a horse's attention. I like to use it prior to physical punishment or discipline on a horse. By using voice warning, I'm giving him a chance to accomplish doing a thing before I hurt him. It has been said that training is punishment and reward. I believe this to an extent. What we are talking about here is to use voice in warning before punishment, and to use punishment less in training. By using voice communication right a lot of the latter can be eliminated. You should also keep your voice low. A horse's hearing is very keen. He can hear things human ears cannot.

Trainers fall into different classes. Professionals, semi-professionals, then there's the man or woman, boy or girl, who is going to try to train his own horses. Nobody knows it all. Everybody can use some sound advice. As far as the word training is concerned, it would apply to any and all schooling of the horse. Let us give some thought to a trainer, including anyone who is trying to train his own horse. Let us see what he should know, or some of what the basic knowledge should be. There is one thing that any person trying to train a horse must have. He must have some kind of communication with the horse.

It takes a certain amount of time to teach a horse that he is being schooled, and in a way going to school with you as his instructor. But after a few sessions of training, perhaps, in the neighborhood of twelve to fifteen sessions and lasting not more than one-half hour to forty-five minutes, and if you use the same area to do it each time, he will soon acquaint the area with the fact that it's here that new things are expected of him. He will start to focus his attention on what you are trying to teach him. In other words, he will alert himself and prepare himself for what's coming.

I think it might be wise to say a few words about the horse's confidence at this point of his career. If you don't over discipline, or get the horse so scared of you he cannot concentrate on what you're trying to get across to him, you should be instilling a certain amount of confidence and trust in the horse's knowledge that you aren't going to hurt him. Then if you let him know by voice and touch, he's doing okay, he should be on the way to accepting the fact that he is in training and give you his full attention.

The age of a colt as to the time he's to start his first saddling and riding sessions is very important. His body and muscles are tender and unused to carrying equipment and a rider's weight on his back. His mouth is tender to the bit. His nose is tender to the hackamore. All these things are strange to him. He should be given considerable time to get used to them. It should be a gradual build-up in process to enable the horse to digest each new thing involved with plenty of time. Time is very important in making the good horse. Too many shortcuts at this point and trying to substitute gimmicks to take the place of time, sometimes keeps a good horse from reaching his peak in capabilities. In my opinion, a colt should not be started before he is a full two years old. You can't expect a child to withstand the strain and stress of training as you would an adult. Nor would you expect primary students to do high school work. The same applies to the horse. Then we get to the size of the two-year-old. Even when the colt is a full two years old and he's not average in comparison to other horses of the same age, I'd wait on him for awhile rather than hurting him or take a chance on his breaking down.

The ideal colt to start riding, if he's a full two years old, would be from eight hundred fifty to a thousand pounds and up. He should be fourteen hands or better tall. A horse that's pretty straight-legged. One that has a long slope to his shoulder. This will allow the saddle to set where it belongs. The short straight shoulder on a horse makes your saddle rigging set too far forward, and your cinch rings will be squeezing into his shoulder muscles. I would also like some withers on him. Some horses are so round withered it's hard to position a saddle on them. If they are both round withered and straight shouldered, they can sure be a problem. Last but not least is a good halter broke colt that has had enough ground work done on him before you start riding him.

Communicating with your Horse

I'm not too high on trying to teach the baby foal while he's still nursing his mother, other than getting your hands on him, scratching him, petting him, and just getting his confidence, so he will trust you and doesn't mind you working around him. This will help later in getting a halter on him and teaching him to lead. It will also help when he's taken off the mother. After that point she no longer takes care of him, and he's going to have to be handled, fed, watered, and exercised by someone.

Teaching a horse requires that he fear you enough to respect you, but at the same time not so fearful that he loses confidence in you. Petting the horse and changes in voice when talking to him are about the only communication you have with the animal. Discipline is of course, included in this. For instance, when you pet the horse, at the same time, speak softly with a little affection in your tone. This soon tells him everything is all right. This is carried along through his schooling when he's doing things in the right way. Then when he's making a mistake we change the tone of our voice. We scold him and the voice should change. Use more authority and perhaps a little threatening in tone. But you must not punish the horse too severely until you're positive he knows he's making a mistake. In other words use mild punishment and mild scolding and threat in voice. Use a more severe tone when you're sure he knows better and is making a mistake. If followed, this little code later on works at whatever you try to teach the horse. It takes some doing to teach a horse to give and keep giving you his full attention. It does not happen overnight. It's like everything you teach him. You start on one thing and don't stop until you know he's getting it through his head and has done it repeatedly fairly well. This, of course, would cover several training sessions. You can now start something else and go back frequently and improve on what he already knows but has not perfected yet. Your voice tone that you have used at the beginning will help draw the horse's attention back to where it belongs. So you can start teaching again. Before you discipline a horse with bat, spurs, or whip, you should use some signal or cue that he's making a mistake. This is what I call always giving him a chance. He will eventually respond to tone of voice to eliminate the discipline that is going to follow. This goes a long way towards building up confidence in the horse's mind.

I think with the baby colt, you cannot over-do babying him, on the average, until after it's been weaned a couple of months. But from that time on some care must be taken that it's not over done. Some colts at this time start to feel you out to see how far they can go and what they can get away with. If this colt resents too much handling at an early age and threatens the handler by kicking or nipping, he is being over-handled and should be left alone for a period of time. But if the colt has to be handled, which may be necessary from time to time, and he starts these mistakes, he's got to be disciplined strong enough to make him stop. If not he is liable to carry these mistakes to maturity, and that will pose a problem later on. Children especially, should be cautioned when to stop pestering a horse to prevent this from happening. If the colt is over-handled when a baby, he is tempted to pay much less attention to a person handling him than one that hasn't. He gets so used to it, he loses interest in everything that goes on. When this type of horse is put into advanced training, the trainer runs into the same problems with him. He has to spend valuable time remaking the horse, to alert him to the fact he's being schooled for something.

People, not in the know, have a habit of scratching the colt's head behind the ears, and giving the colt sugar at different times in handling him. The big mistake they make with stud colts of all ages is rubbing or scratching the muzzle of the colt. It isn't long before the colt takes this as a game and starts to nip. He develops a liking for sugar and he starts to expect and look for tidbits at any and all times. I think if given at a certain time of day and not repeated in between it's okay. But to start the colt expecting and looking for goodies all the time is a mistake. You'll not get his attention for other things while his attention is being focused on this one thing, meaning sugar, carrots or other treats.

Whatever part of a subject we are trying to teach the horse, let us take a look at how and when we should bring the voice aid again into the picture. From the beginning do not talk to the horse all the time. Use your voice only when you are rewarding him for achievement or disciplining him for mistakes. The tone should be soft, not excited or loud, and limited to a few words. Use words such as "good boy," "good girl," or "fine," "okay," or "good." Then follow with a pat or rub on his neck, or any place on the horse's body except his head. Leave it alone. The less you touch his head the better off you are. Don't scratch him around his nose or don't scratch behind his ears. This is what starts horses to nipping and biting and could also start a colt on the way to being head shy.

If you use this tone of voice in a limited way, the horse soon learns that it is a reward, and along with the pat he knows he's going in the right direction in his training. But remember you only use the soft tone when he's doing okay. You use voice tone just the opposite when you catch the horse in a mistake, or when you see he's starting to make one.

I think another important factor along with voice and touch by way of communication is your eye contact with that of a horse. If you will take time to observe where the colt's eyes are focusing on you, especially when the first time you work with him on something new to him, you will find the main focus of his eyes will be directly into your eyes. He won't be looking at your feet or your body but right into your eyes. If you would ask trainers where they are looking while teaching a horse on the ground, they would most likely reply that they would be looking the horse in the eye most of the time, regardless of what they would be doing with their hands or body. But they maybe would not be able to explain why they do. I think there is a lot to this. I'm not suggesting that it's a form of hypnotism, but I'm sure there is a contact. I believe a horse has an inherent quality to determine from looking into your eyes what your intentions might be as far as whether you're going to hurt him or not. I'd go further in saying whether your attitude is hostile towards him or not. I have to believe that this is one of the reasons some pretty capable horsemen never excell as trainers, or why some men can do things with spooky horses without spooking or shaking them up. Where some have difficulty communicating with the same horse. It's sure worth a try and could be one of the hidden magics some people think some trainers have. I think I first found it out working with bronc horses on the ground. I believed I watched his eyes for an indication of his moves in order

14

to protect myself. But through the years I've never stopped it. So it must have served a purpose. If you asked trainers who had broke and worked a lot of horses, they would probably answer, "I think I do watch their eyes but never gave much thought as to why I do this." I've never read any material about this in relation to horse training. Also we can add here, that you can sure see when a horse is mad or real scared when observing his eyes. I've seen horses' eyes when real shook up, change colors to the extent that their eyes become almost smokey in appearance, and on viewing his eyes when he settled down could see a positive difference in the color.

His ears are also to be watched when you are on him. If he's giving you his complete attention, most of the time you will see the holes in his ears facing you or one at least. If he drops one ear and repeats it, you can just about figure something is wrong on that side where he tilted his ear. You should dismount and look him over. He might have picked up a stone or your cinch might be binding some hair under it, especially when you first mount him. The ears when pinned back mean the horse is mad or angry. This is a warning that he might bite, wheel and kick. You will also see roping, dogging, and cutting horses do it when working cattle. I think in these instances, it's a little anger and determination thrown in. Anyway, two things can be said here. Watch his eyes and ears when on the ground and especially his ears when you're on him. They can tell you a lot. When you're not on him, and he's on his own, and not studying or looking at an object, his ears will be straight up, but will be with the hole in the ear to the side. He can get a better range of hearing both front and rear and to the side in this manner.

The horse is also able to detect and determine a lot from his sense of smell. I believe a human, when really scared, gives off a certain scent that makes a horse react. The same applies to the handler or trainer. If he is mad or hostile towards the animal, I think the horse can detect it from scent. I think he accepts the controlled fear scent in a man quicker than others. If he realizes you're a little afraid of him, it helps him accept your handling of him. If your movements are steady and controlled, his fear of you lessens as he realizes you're a little afraid of him also.

Your actions handling green horses should be slow, smooth, and deliberate. You should make a practice of it. You can by constant attention make a practice of it where it's almost an art. This gives the horse an opportunity to watch every move you make. When he

15

doesn't see any sudden moves on your part, it will help him to understand you aren't going to do anything to harm him. This will help build up confidence in him. As your tension subsides his fear of you will also subside. In a short while you will have confidence in each other. There are more wrong or bad moves made by horses because of fear of you than any other reason. Let him retain a little fear of you. Just enough to make him want to do your bidding. Your encouragement at every little success on his part will make him want to please you more. A lot of good common sense on your part will go a long ways towards your improvement in your schooling of the horse. Never fail to start lessons that are easy for him to understand. Don't expect him to do hard things or learn them in his first lessons. If you try to teach him difficult things too early, and he fails to accomplish them, he will be less willing or eager to learn the easy ones as well. In my opinion, one of the greatest assets the horse has is his memory. Unfortunately, he also remembers the bad things as well as the good. He reacts accordingly. If a trainer repeatedly makes a blunder this, too, remains in the horse's memory, and is sometimes hard to overcome.

 **3**

Haltering and Leading the Colt

Halter breaking, from necessity, is the first step in the training of a colt. When I start to halter break a colt I like to start with a colt that has been weaned. I don't like to fool around with a colt trying to put a halter on him or trying to teach him to lead while he's still on the mare. I'd rather have him off the mare for about a week. The situations vary, of course, and it might have to be done sooner to take care of the youngster. The reason I'd wait is that the colt will do little else but worry and call to his mother for a few days. These stages he's going through will sure not help him pay attention to his trainer or handler. So assuming that he's settled down and eating fairly well, we'll start to halter break this colt. The choice of a halter here is important. Use a stout one as on any age horse you're going to halter break. Once you have the colt haltered, and it being the problem that it is to get it on, one of your more difficult tasks has been accomplished. The halter should be strong enough so that it does not break when you start to tie the colt up solid for the first time. Also care must be taken in its adjustment. If the nose band on the halter hangs too low under the jaw, a stout pull or jerk will pull it up over the top of his nose and cause you to have to start over. It may result in his getting loose. You do not want it too tight either. This will cause the colt some discomfort and will probably skin him up and make him sore. This will result in the colt becoming very sensitive to your touch, making him fear you when you are trying to handle him in that area. So spend a little time, do the adjusting properly. This will keep the halter on him. I am assuming that you are going to be keeping the colt penned up or in a stall while you are teaching him to lead. My preference in getting a halter on the colt would be to do this in a stall. But in the actual teaching of the colt to lead, my preference would be in a corral or pen free of obstacles. You should pick a place to do this job where if for any reason, he jerks away from you, he cannot get too far. In an alley of a set of stalls is all right if all doors are closed. A good corral or pen free from barb wire is all right, too. Barb wire, incidentally, is the horse's worst enemy. Don't try to train horses in any place where it is present. Some of the things that happen to people when halter breaking colts are: (1) the colt goes over backwards, strikes his head on the ground or rocks. Sometimes killing it, or if not outright killing him, he suffers some brain damage that shows up later on in his life. (2) The colt will get away because the trainer is not working in an enclosed area. The colt at this time looks around, sees and feels a lead rope flapping and dangling around his body. He goes crazy from fear and runs at or into whatever is in front of him. The result is body injuries, vet bills that cost a lot of money, and time with nothing thus far accomplished but an injured animal. So the saying about "prevention" would sure help a lot here. In other words "think" before you start this procedure.

Use an eight-foot or longer lead rope. Make sure your halter fits the colt. Work in an enclosed area with no doors or gates left open, and no loose items such as old machinery, junk, or other materials that could hurt your colt. A word about halters. If for any reason you would turn a horse or a colt out where he cannot be caught up for a few days or checked periodically, take his halter off. He can get hung up in trees, steel fence posts, caught in wire or if it's a web or rope halter, and it rains, the halter can shrink enough where it can hurt or injure the horse's head. Play it safe. Also, look your stall over for any hooks or boards that he might get hung up on with his halter.

I'm going to give you a brief description of how I think a colt that is good halter broke should function. If he's been taught to watch your hands and the lead rope that is in it, he will turn right or left when he feels the slightest pressure on his nose from the halter nose band. He will follow you on a loose lead rope and will turn when you turn, trot when you trot, stop when you stop. He will not root his nose up and out when you are trying to turn or run over you when you stop. These things are what I call being light in the halter. You hear about a horse being light in the hackamore or being light in the bridle. The starting of a horse being light in the hackamore or bridle is being light in the halter. You have heard these expressions, I'm sure.

In the early stages when attempting to get this colt to lead or follow you, the one thing to avoid is pulling straight ahead on that lead rope. Common sense tells you that you cannot drag three hundred pounds or more of horseflesh behind you if he wants to resist. So what you will do is move out at a forty-five-degree angle off to one side of this colt. Have your lead rope loose, get the colt's attention, hold your hands waist high so he can see them. Then command him with your voice saying sharp and clear, "Come here." Then give this lead rope a sharp little jerk and follow through with a steady pull making the colt take one step sideways and come off center in front. At this point loosen your pressure or pull on the lead rope. Go up to him, reward him in a gentle tone, scratch his neck, loosen the halter from around his ears. Don't scratch his ears, just push up on the halter. Even though it is loose, it will move off the nerve center, the spot directly behind his ears. He gets a certain amount of relief from it. The next move will be to the opposite side at the same forty-five-degree angle. Repeat on the other side the exact things you did on the first side. Remember a little jerk, enough to hurt his nose a little, on the top not his jaw, to draw his attention to the lead rope in our hands. Follow through with a pull, keeping your hands where he can see them "waist high." When the pull and the sidestep of the colt has been made, go to him, speak softly, pat, and repeat the same procedure on the other side. This will be done about eight or nine times. Start to watch this colt's reaction in the following manner—When you give him the voice command, "Come here," and your hands are ready for the jerk and pull, hesitate, give a second command, "Come here." If no indication is given on the colt's part that he's going to move toward the forty-five-degree angle in line with your body, jerk a little harder. He will look towards the lead rope and your hands to see where the pressure is coming from. It won't be long before he will be making the sidesteps at your command on his own. At the first time you notice even an inclination in that direction on his part, and this is important, make a big thing out of it, to let him know that this is the message you are trying to get across. When he's making these sidesteps pretty freely, you can go a few feet straight ahead of him. Use the command, "Come here." Pull lightly but don't jerk. It won't be long before he will be following you. If he doesn't, go back to the forty-five-degree angle pull. But instead of going back to the opposite side, go another forty-five degrees into the circle until he is bending around with you on a light pull.

The trainer should keep in mind that the length of time taken on these halter breaking sessions is important. Don't make lessons so long at this time that the colt becomes weary of focusing his attention on the training. Limit your actual schooling sessions. The colt's attention to you will be sharp the first one-half hour you work with him. It will get less from that time on. Take a step at a time. Be direct and repeat every move you make alike. Once you know the colt understands what you are trying to get across to him, don't keep after him too long on that session. Start over again with it when his mind is fresh. Here again are the don'ts: (1) Don't allow enough slack in your lead rope that the movements of the colt in his reaction to what you are doing, enable him to get his leg or legs over the lead rope. (2) Keep it high enough off the ground at all times. (3) Do not pull straight ahead on the colt, always at an angle. This will give you some leverage. Make sure the colt is watching you before you jerk or pull sideways. Study him all the time. The first time you observe that he's starting to get the message, reward him by voice and touch. Start again. Give him a chance to respond before jerking on that lead rope and the pull. After the colt is following you on a fairly loose lead rope and if he's turning to the right or left with your movements he is making good progress.

This has probably covered three different training sessions, and the colt should be about ready to be tied up. Do not tie this colt up and leave him tied, unless you are going to be there to watch him, and for not more than one-half hour to an hour for at least three different sessions. Pick a spot to tie him that will hold him. Be sure that you tie him high enough that he will not pull his neck down. The height should be about eight inches or a foot above the height of his withers. Make sure all nails and loose materials in front of the colt are removed, because after setting back on his halter and pulling back, he will no doubt lunge ahead into whatever is in front of him. The length of the tie from the post to the halter should not be too long. If he comes up high with his front quarters, he will almost for sure get a front leg over it. This brings to mind about the kind of knot to use. A slip knot that can be pulled out or a Bowline knot that won't come tight would be what you would use. Another method is with a long enough lead rope, so that you can take a wrap around the top of the post. Then stand far enough away from the animal so if he gets in trouble, such as throwing himself, coming up high in front, getting a front leg over the rope all you have to do is to give him some slack on the wrap until you get him straightened out and start the procedure once more. For the first time that the colt is tied solid this method is my preference. Once he has quit fighting, he can then be tied without the risk that would have been taken had the colt been tied with a knot the first time.

In conclusion on these first sessions on halter breaking the young colt, let me state that there are other aids that can be used in this part of his schooling in halter training. But for me I have found it to be the most convincing to the colt that he's expected to lead and that he has no alternatives but to do so.

I will add a reminder here. The direction of the movements of the hands on working the lead rope, especially on the side jerk and pull, should always be in a down direction because you want the pull on the top of the nose and not on the lower jaw.

We have gone to some length and detail to describe the way to halter break a colt. We have assumed that this type of colt had been nursed by a gentle mare. Now let us say that we have come up against a different type colt. Supposing we bought a colt that was wild, unhandled, and never had a halter on it. We would have to apply different measures to get a halter on this type colt. One way would be to take a catch rope and rope the animal around the neck. This should be done in a small pen or corral that was built well enough that the colt could not jump over it or go through it.

Once the colt is roped and has felt the loop tighten around his neck, he will react. At this time do not set down on your rope or try to stop the colt, providing the pen is small enough where he can't get too far in any direction while dragging the rope. Your next move would be to hold the rope high enough where he won't get his feet over it. It won't be long before the colt will adjust to the loop around his neck. You can then start to pull towards your body, forcing the colt to face you. Then you can start hand over hand on the rope, little by little, to get close enough to the animal to get one hand on his neck. Scratch and pet him to the point where he will stand without choking him down. It will not be long before you can ease the halter on him.

If you cannot rope I would advise against this method. A

squeeze pen or a chute could also be used to accomplish this objective.

Advanced Haltering

Let us say after reviewing what we have so far covered in the haltering and handling in our efforts to teach the colt to lead, we have progressed to the point that he is following us fairly well. He has gotten through his mind that he is to turn when you turn, stop when you stop, and is standing quietly when you're standing still. He has been tied up solid and has pulled back enough times and failed at getting away or loose from what he has been tied to. He has accepted the fact that he has been unable to gain any advantage by using all the strength he has. The tieing up process has defeated any and all attempts on his part to gain his freedom.

Our efforts shall now be concentrated on furthering this horse's halter and leading ability. One way I've found that worked well for me was to take a piece of rope about fifteen feet long. A rope that is seven-sixteenths in diameter and soft in texture. I would secure one end of this rope around the neck of the horse in about the same position that the throat latch of my bridle head stall would be. The rope should not be tight around the neck, but not real loose either. Use a knot that will not allow the rope to tighten up to impair the horse's breathing or choke him. A Bowline knot is fine or just a good square knot is okay. You also would have your halter on the colt for this part of your training. After securing one end of your rope around the horse's or colt's neck run the other loose end of this rope under the throat latch part of your halter. Then make one single half-hitch in your rope and slip it over the colt's muzzle. The half-hitch should go in behind and under the nose band on the halter then around the nose. Adjust this loop to where it sets up under the nose band of the halter. The top of the loop should be on the bridge of the horse's nose about where a hackamore would set.

I'm sure that there are other ways to get this done, other than that of which I am going to describe, but I doubt if there are any that can get it done quicker or will convince the colt more conclusively that he has to do it. This method will work on all horses of all ages and will improve many horses that have the habit of lugging back on the halter while being led.

We now have our rope securely around the colt or horse's neck. We have adjusted it to where we can slip our hand between his neck and the rope, in other words where it's comfortable and not irritating him. It might be wise to point out at this time that we will at no time tie this animal up with this piece of equipment that we are about to use. Its sole purpose is to improve his obedience and performance in leading. So that this horse will be a pleasure to lead and perhaps help set him up for a later showing at halter. Which some of you will no doubt want to do.

The adjustment of this piece of equipment is simple. Once you have the single loop up under the nose band on the halter, fit it where there isn't any slack between that part of the rope that goes around the animal's neck and the single loop that sets around his nose. The secret of this method and its results are its action in teaching the horse that if the lead rope doesn't tighten, he will experience no pain. As long as he's on a loose lead, he can avoid

Proper adjustment of rope to induce horse to lead better

Photography by Neil Mishler, Ponca, Nebraska

getting pinched or hurt.

I will now proceed to tell you readers how to put this method into operation. Go back to the way we originally instructed you on the forty-five degree angle, one of the first steps taken in teaching the animal to lead. Number one to its success is to make positively sure that the half-hitch around the horse's nose is not tight before any attempt is made to put this method into action. Care should be taken to acquaint the horse with this new method gradually. Do not expect to do the whole bit on the first session of its use. Introduce its first use and effect by going forty-five degrees to the right or to the left of the animal. Get his attention with the voice command, "Come here." Then if he doesn't respond give this lead rope a sharp little jerk or snap. When this horse reacts by moving forward, loosen your lead rope by giving him some slack. Then coil up your lead rope, and go to the horse and loosen that loop around his nose. Speak encouragingly to him and pat him on the neck. Then go to the opposite side and repeat what you did on the former side. You will soon find this horse will be turning and coming to you. He will also be watching that rope so that it does not tighten, thus hurting his nose. This same method applies to get him to move forward more rapidly. He will get to know that if the lead rope is loose, he will not get hurt. Every time he respons favorably, go to the animal and loosen that loop that has tightened up around his nose. This is his reward. Once this horse has had this method used on him enough to where he's really watching and doing every thing well, you can discontinue its use and he will function the same with only the halter and lead rope.

Looking back on what I've written, I find that there are some precautions you beginners might keep in mind. Do not at any time take a wrap around your hand with a lead rope. The horse you are handling might get the upper hand and take off. If you cannot free your hand, you could be dragged and seriously injured. I know of one case where a young girl got killed in this manner. I also knew a grown man to lose a thumb the same way. Take every advantage you can. Don't take any more chances than you have to. Most, but not all, accidents handling horses can be avoided if you can learn to think while handling them using the right precautions. It's also my opinion that young horses worked with the method I've just described take to their early hackamore training much better and quicker. They will also learn to work much easier on a lunge line. (Which I will cover later on in this book.) Everything you do with the young horse in its early handling, and the methods you use will almost for a certainty influence the animal in your final goal, which is to have a good performance horse.

Riding and Training Equipment

Saddles

One of the more important things in a person's endeavor to ride and school a horse is equipment that will fit the horse. The knowledge of what it would consist of, and most important is how to adjust and use it.

Let us start with saddles. There are a lot of good saddles on the market. My preference for a training saddle would be a saddle that's been broke in with the squeaks out of it. It should have a full double or seven-eighths double rigging and not a cheap one. It should have a thirteen to fourteen-inch swell with a little undercut for grip. I like the double billet on the right side, and I like a good wide latigo on the left side. I would then take a leather punch and punch an extra hole between the holes already in it. Do this with both billet and latigo. Most manufacturers fail to put enough holes in this particular part of their equipment. At times when you're cinching that horse up, that extra hole means a lot when you're trying to place a saddle just right on him.

I do not like any dish in my saddle as I like to ride my balance and have found that setting in a hole makes it harder for me to get my weight up off the horse's loins. It also helps in my ability to have free leg movements forward and backward. I like to use a wide, back flank cinch, and a good, strong, soft, flat bar cinch in front with tongues on both ends. Examine your old billet and latigo. Don't take chances on this part of your equipment when riding any horses. Your connecting strap between rear and front girth should be looked at to make sure no rivets or leather lacing is gouging your horse. The cantle on the saddle to my way of liking is about a three-inch Cheyenne roll cantle. I also like the wide deep type ropers stirrups to train with. I can get more balance in them. I can get off a lot faster and easier if I get in a storm, than the narrower type. Another thing I find to my advantage is the fact I can mount a green horse easier with them. Last, but not least, people buy roping saddles when they aren't ropers and probably never will be. I think they should think about this before they buy a saddle. When you are learning to ride or schooling a green horse, this is important.

I like the full quarter horse bars on a saddle. They fit better and lower on the round withered colt. They can also be built up on the higher withered horse by adding more blankets. One thing you should check is the gullet of your saddle. After you have cinched up your saddle make sure the top of the gullet is not resting down on the withers of the horse. You should be able to have at least one inch or more visible between your blanket and the top of the saddle gullet.

If your stirrups are not trained out, a quick way to train them out is to set your saddle on a bale of hay. Take two five-gallon pails of water and place each stirrup in each pail of water. Let them soak about two hours. Then remove them from the water and twist the soaked fenders to the front of the stirrup leather. Tie them with a piece of bale twine just above your stirrup. Place your saddle on a saddle rack. Then put a broom handle or pitchfork handle through the stirrups and leave them there overnight. One application of this is enough as a rule, but you won't have to repeat it over twice. This will save you from having to fish for that off side stirrup when mounting the green colt. Don't try to reach over as you have seen a lot of people do to straighten or position your foot in that stirrup. On some horses you will wind up on your head and have a loose horse.

Another thing you might do even on a new saddle or an old one, is check for nails. I'm not a saddle maker, but I have pulled a lot of nails out of the sheepskin lining on saddles. The heads of these nails were protruding out all the way from one-eighth to one-half inch from the level of the lining of the saddle. I think they place nails in the saddle to hold that particular piece in place while working or finishing them. Then they either forget to remove the nails or neglect to do so. Anyway, run your hand over the surface and if you locate one remove it. You can almost imagine what the colt is going to feel and do if it gouges him.

One other thing I'd forgotten to mention here is to also punch more holes in the back billets. You will use them to a good advantage when you want your rear girth to be in the exact center of your horse's belly.

We have covered saddles pretty well. My main idea was to get across to the reader some of these points about saddles: (1) the comfort of the horse; (2) by using the right kind it might improve the rider's ability in training his mount.

The patented buckles that are put on these stirrup leathers where they used to be strictly laced are okay. But you have sure got to take a look at where they rub on the side of your horse. When your stirrups are trained out this twists the buckle where if you don't position it right in your adjustment, you will find it's gouging your horse from the movement of your leg. It won't be long before it's raw where it's rubbing. You will be wondering what is causing your horse to act so funny.

Now, about the extra or half holes the saddle makers don't put in their saddle stirrup leathers. One inch too long or one inch too short will cause a rider to be out of balance and in the wrong position to set a horse right. All you have to do is go to a horse show where there are quite a bunch of horsemen. You will see some of them not riding balance because they are riding too short of a stirrup and pushing ahead on these stirrups. This makes them set flat down on their horse. Then others will be riding too long of a stirrup not enabling the rider to get up in his stirrups. This also makes him set down on his horse. This can be eliminated by putting your saddle on a gentle horse. Then get aboard the horse. The correct position you are trying to seek is, with your legs bent slightly at the knees, and your legs down and back in line with your thighs, stand up, and you should now be about one and one-half inches off your saddle. If not, put that extra hole in your stirrup leather so you can be in this position. Because when you're riding balance western style and in time with the movements of your horse, you will feel it. It's also the most comfortable position. Besides, it puts your legs in the right position later when you want to use leg cues on the horse.

Hackamore

The piece of head gear I'm going to recommend using on a young horse when first starting to ride him is the hackamore. I strongly advise its use for a two-month period of time before

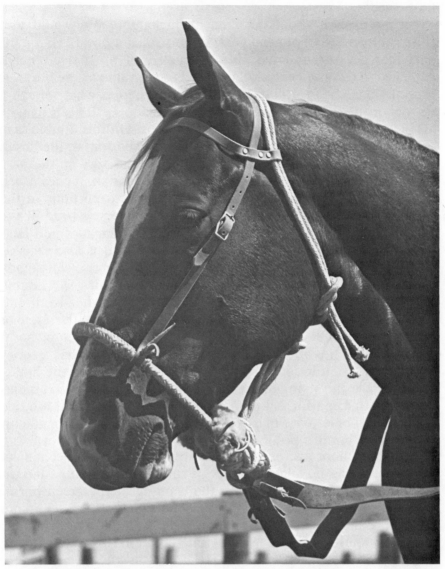

Complete made-up hackamore with sheepskin protection

Photography by Nell Mishler, Ponca, Nebraska

bitting the green horse with a ring snaffle bit. The hackamore can be used for most of the basics on the horse during this period of training. If used, it will be instrumental in preserving the horse's mouth. An old saying that's true, in part at least, is, "No mouth, no horse."

Let me explain about the kind of hackamore you would use. It's a complete piece of head gear. It consists of a bosal. That's the part that goes around the nose or muzzle of the horse's head. Attached to this is a head stall fastened to each side of the bosal. It is not unlike a head stall on a bridle. Then there is what we call a fiadore or the cowboy expressed word "Theadore." This is usually made from a piece of doubled sash cord rope. On this double sash cord there's a hackamore knot that fits on the bottom of the bosal. It is enclosed around a ball that's plaited and sets at the very bottom of the bosal. Then above this knot about six inches a bell knot is made. Here the sash cord separates. Two portions of the rope go up and around behind the ears of the horse's head at the poll and comes on over the top of his head and engages in a loop formed on the bell knot to create a throat latch. It is also secured to the head stall at the top by a brow band that has two slots made on each side. Your headstall goes through one slot. The double rope of the fiadore goes through the other holding headstall and fiadore together. It is similiar to a halter. This is the type of hackamore you will concern yourself with. The finishing type bosal differs from it. It is only the bosal and headstall. It also has a series of wraps to give it weight to drop away from the jaw of the horse. But as we are only going to use the hackamore to start the colt and finish him in a snaffle and curb or grazing bit, we will not use this kind on our horse. We will use only the full and complete made up fiadore and bosal type of hackamore.

The hackamore bit, or sometimes referred to as a mechanical hackamore, has no place in the green horse's training. It is a hindrance rather than an aid in the training of the green horse.

The reason more young horses are not started in the hackamore in this day and age is, in my opinion, people do not understand or know how to use one. So I'm going into detail in this writing to try to give you more specifics about it. When you buy a hackamore, here is what you would ask for at your western store. You want a hackamore with a fiadore on it. In other words a throat latch. Don't buy one that has a steel cable in the center. They are too severe even in experienced hands.

The bosal that is braided throughout is pliable and can be shaped, and must be if it's new. It is the best one to use. After you've purchased this hackamore, soak the bosal part of it in water for several hours. Then take a gallon can and put the bosal on the can. Push the adjusting clip at the bottom as close to the can as you can. Leave the bosal on the can until it dries. After it has been on the can for an hour, check the adjusting loop making sure that it's forced up as close to the can as possible. One of the big mistakes made by the average person after they purchase the hackamore is not shaping it by soaking it prior to using. You cannot soak and shape the bosal that has the steel cable in it. After the bosal has been soaked and shaped on the can, it will eliminate the pinch on the horse's lower jaw. This pinch on the jaw is in direct contrast to the effect we're trying to achieve on the horse's muzzle. We want to eliminate this pressure or as much as possible, on the lower jaw, and apply this pressure to the bridge of the horse's nose. The unshaped bosal, even though it does not have the steel core, will pinch almost as much as the one that does.

After shaping and removing this hackamore from the can, take a piece of sheepskin about four by four inches and place it in the V at the lower part of the hackamore. Your next step will be to secure the sheepskin in the V. It can be done by cutting a small slit in two or three places on each side of the sheepskin. So that it can be tied off with small lace leather around each side of the bottom of the hackamore. The protection of the horse's jaw from the hackamore is important. If you sore the skin on the jaw of the colt, you will be giving him a definite reason to raise his head away from any pull on the reins. This you are trying to avoid. The last step is to put your reins on the hackamore.

I like to use two latigos for reins on a complete made up hackamore in my first riding of a green colt. I attach them to the Bosal below the fiador knot of the hackamore. These latigo reins are about one and one-half inches wide, and are the type of latigo that is used on the lighter and cheaper saddles. They can be purchased at most tack shops. I like these wide reins on green horses as you can get a better hold on them. Also, another main function is you'll be tieing the colt's head around before riding, and the latigo rein is much easier to go through the latigos and billet when you are in the process of doing so. They also sell some braided hackamore reins made out of cotton rope. If you want to change to these reins later on, you can.

I've used the hackamore on every green horse I have started. I've taken some bad mouthed spoiled horses, and started from scratch with them using the hackamore. I was successful in changing a lot of unmanageable horses into horses that turned out to be at least usable riding horses. These horses had been punished by the wrong use of bits in their early training. Their mouths had been wrecked by mishandling. After finding these facts out, it further inspired my use of the hackamore to avoid it. My knowing the advantages of the hackamore's use, and my trying to get it across to more horsemen to use the hackamore; I think I will have done something for the horses as well as the people that own them.

Now let me give some advice to the not too knowledgeable horseman. We will start with the area in which you intend to do your riding of the animal. The first five or six saddlings should take place in a round or square corral not more than forty feet by forty feet in size. A smaller one is all right, but a larger one is not advisable. We are talking about a corral or breaking pen to first ride the colt in. This will give the rider an advantage. It's about the right size to lunge a horse in, which I will cover later. Another advantage is the fact that should the horse buck or you get in a storm, the colt will not be able to get away. When we are talking about the corral, it should be about six feet tall and made out of lumber, two by six's or two by eight's. It should be stout enough to hold him. You can get more done in this small pen in a week or two in getting a horse started than you could in a month in a larger area unless you are a pretty good hand with a horse and know what you're doing.

If I were a novice, I would use that small pen for as long as it took to get the horse side reining with a rein in each hand. I would also make sure this horse was stopping on "whoa" or a neck and pull cue before venturing out into a larger arena. With your limited knowledge of the hackamore that you will be using, I'd not do the following things: I would not go out where there's traffic. I would not go where there was barb wire, I would not go on rough or rocky ground. I would not go where there was old machinery, junk cars, or old lumber piles. In fact, I'd have the horse bitted and pretty well broke before I left the breaking pen and arena to go to any outside area.

There are many places where you can take your horse and board him. A lot of them have inside arenas where you can get this training job done. Take all the advantage you can of the situation, and lessen your chances of hurting yourself or your horse.

Snaffle Bit

We should have started and finished the basics on this horse while in the hackamore, before we bit him with the snaffle bit. I suggest that he be doing the following things basically in the hackamore within a two-month period. He should stand quietly when being saddled. He should not resist us when exchanging the halter for the hackamore. Then after leading him off center for a couple minutes, stand still when we mount him. He should wait on us to give him a signal to move forward after we have gathered up our reins. The latter is accomplished by not letting him move out while you're mounting him. Try to make the horse stand at least a few seconds after mounting. He should walk out on a slack rein. He should not attempt to trot or lope until asked to do so. He should do each of these things only when cued to do so. When the left rein is rested against the left side of his neck in front of the shoulder, he should turn his nose immediately to the right and follow through with his front quarters. He should do the same thing in the same way when neck reined to the left. He should be taking several steps back fairly straight. He should pick up each individual lead from a slow trot.

There are several different snaffle bits on the market. I like an aluminum D ring snaffle or a straight round ring snaffle bit. They come in all prices. There are some that would say they would not use any kind of bit that was not steel, but I like the aluminum ones because they are light in weight. I have never had any problems with them, or the steel ones for that matter. I don't think it makes all that much difference. I would buy the slotted round rubber guards to prevent pinching the corners of the horse's mouth. I also tie the bit up. It's important that the young horse when first bitted does not get the habit of running his tongue over the bit at the first pressure put on the bit. This is the first thing he tries to do. Once he forms the habit, it is very hard to correct. When he does have his tongue over the bit instead of under it and pressure is applied to the reins, the pressure is put on the hinge under his tongue. This causes head tossing horses, runaway horses and a horse who will not pay any attention to what you are trying to teach him.

For training the young horse I would get a plain kind of a stout headstall. I have never liked split ear headstalls for training. I like a brow band with the buckle on the left side of the headstall for adjustment. Get a wide leather headstall with a throat latch on it. The horse cannot rub this kind off.

There are two methods that I use to tie the bit up on a green horse. Number one: Leave his halter on. Bridle the horse. Adjust the headstall and bit so that the bit is just barely resting against the bars and corners of the horse's mouth. A slight wrinkle at the corners of the horse's mouth is permissible, but no more than that. Take a piece of short leather thong about a foot long. Tie one end of the thong to the top of the snaffle. Take this thong and make three wraps around the nose band of the halter. Spread the wraps so that they go across the bridge of the nose of the horse. Then tie the other end of the thong to the other ring of the snaffle bit. Examine what you've done to make sure that both sides of the thong have made contact so that it supports the snaffle bit. Just enough to keep the weight of the bit off the horse's tongue. This will keep him from running his tongue over the bit in the early stages of his training. Make sure when you are using this method that you have adjusted the halter so that the nose band of the halter is resting on the bridge of the horse's nose or a little higher. This will put the thong that you tied the bit up with in the proper position.

The other method of tying the bit up without the use of the halter is to take a curb chain with a tie strap on each end. Run this chain from ring to ring of the bit over the bridge of the horse's nose. To hold this curb chain in position on the bridge of the horse's nose, take a small piece of leather lacing. Tie one end to the center of the brow band of the headstall. Secure the other end to the exact center of the curb chain. Adjust it in length to where the chain is on the bridge of the horse's nose.

Let me point out to the reader that there will be a similarity to the action of the hackamore in relation to the snaffle bit with the bit tied up. The reaction of the horse to the pull on the rein of the snaffle bit is associated by the horse with the hackamore because the pull on the rein instead of being completely on the bit is a good deal on his nose. Which he is familiar with from his hackamore training. So his graduation from the hackamore to the snaffle is accepted much more readily than if this method is not used. You will find this horse will be far ahead of another horse where this procedure has not been used. He will in a short time be working in the snaffle as good or better than he did in the hackamore. At the same time his mouth is still like velvet. You can come out of that snaffle, meaning the ring type, and go into a swivel jaw snaffle with no problem. It still might be wise to tie the loose shank snaffle up for awhile, too. It can be done in the same manner described above. We won't get into hand position or martingales as I intend to put them in later.

A word about the chin strap. You can put one under your snaffle but make sure it's loose. Its main function is to keep the bit from being pulled through his mouth. At the beginning, when you put your horse in the snaffle, put your reins on top of this chin strap. Remember it is not too important as you already have a tie over his nose. This tie will not allow the bit to come through his mouth. By the reins being on the top of the chin strap, you will not be making your horse come up with his head. From the beginning, when we start riding the colt, we are not going to give him any reason to raise his head. At least we are not going to train it up. We are going to train it down or try hard to get this job done. Horses' high head positions are due a lot to his handling, and the positioning of the hands at some time or other in his training period. Also the use of or mishandled head equipment. Even the beginning horseman, by adhering to a few basic principles, can do a lot for the high headed horse, if they follow the instructions.

I have to give English riding people due credit for perhaps more in this direction than average western riders. I think as a whole, they have had and paid more attention to the hand positions. I think, however, the performance of the western horse in some areas demands a higher head position than that of an English performance horse. The exception might be in their jumping horse. Here you can see the horse given almost complete head freedom as required in his ability to take high and wide jumps.

Spurs and Bat and Their Use

Spurs as an aid to training and starting the western horse, in my opinion, are a necessity in any advanced stages of his training. They are a help, and it's proven by the number of western riders using them. A lot of horses once schooled with spurs perform correctly enough where spurs can be left off most of the time, but the rider will find that once in awhile he has to go back to them to remind and refreshen the horse's memory to get the best out of him. On some horses you have to use spurs all the time if they are inclined to be lazy.

One other piece of equipment that's widely used is the short popper bat. This has taken the place of what they used to call the quirt which was about the same length as the bat. It was made of plaited rawhide with two or three short lashes on the end. It had a thong that slipped over and around the wrist. The modern day bat also has the wrist thong. I have found the bat and its use valuable in the early day stages of the green horse's training, up and through the neck reining stage. But like spurs, it can be overused. Some horses that are spirited will get to where they look back and watch that hand carrying the bat too much. This sometimes will cause a horse to pay more attention to the bat hand and a lot less focus of attention on what you are trying to teach him.

Horses taught to neck rein by a trainer who uses two reins in one hand and the bat in the other will, in my opinion, be doing it wrong. You will find that these horses, though they neck rein fairly well, their head position will be wrong. The following will be noticed: When the horse is being neck reined to the left, instead of the nose going into the turn or straight where it belongs, he will have his nose and the lower part of his head sticking out to the right. The same thing will happen when the horse is being reined to the right. His nose will be sticking out to the left. In other words he's gotten in the habit of watching the bat hand instead of concentrating on the reins.

Another factor that induces this wrong head position is not using a rein in each hand to teach the horse to neck rein. I'll get into that later on in neck reining the horse. One other thing worth mentioning here, and it is important. Most training is done with a rein in each hand whether with a hackamore or a snaffle bit on the horse if it's done right.

It's easy to realize you can't use a rein in each hand when you're trying to use a bat. A limited use of the bat is okay, but some care must be taken as with the use of spurs not to overuse it.

There are many spurs on the market. A lot of horsemen have a preference, but my advice to those just starting to use them is to buy a blunt rowel spur, never a sharp rowel spur. A man that has worn spurs most of his life on ranch horses could probably get away with using a sharp rowel spur. But average unschooled riders have no business using them. To get away from knocking or cutting down any company's design or type, I'll just say all spurs. If they have a sharp pointed rowel don't use them. You should also tape the rowels when riding colts. Some black ordinary electrician's tape will do the trick. Start taping around the rowel and keep on putting on enough tape so that no steel is hitting your horse at any point.

One way you can get used to wearing spurs is to wear them a couple of hours a day when you're doing chores or odd jobs. When you can walk without hooking your pant legs or when you don't trip on either foot you're learning to walk with your feet fairly straight as you would be riding a horse. People that use them should keep in mind that because they have them on doesn't mean they have to be spurring the horse all the time. Use them only when you need them. Then there are those riders I call tickers. They are continually, lightly ticking the horse in the belly with both spurs. It's a mistake. He will learn to build up an immunity to them. This causes the rider to really have to gouge the horse to get any response. Once in awhile you will run into such a dead head horse, you might really have to gouge him to wake him up. A bat might work better on this kind of a horse.

Spurs leave the trainer's hands free which is sure the biggest advantage the rider has. This enables him to control the horse's head at all times, as he has to be really handy with his hands to attain any outstanding work on a green horse, and also later in advanced training.

Raw steel against a colt's belly when it is overused can make or help make a horse into a ring tail. However, it's caused, in my opinion, from other things as well. I think if a horse has bad conformation problems, especially the hocks or in the hind leg area, this is another contributing factor. Also the high-strung horse is more susceptible to it than the other doggie type horse.

Much has been written by horsemen about leg pressure as a means to get the animal to gather up and collect by bringing the hindquarters up under him prior to the execution of an action, such as stopping, pivoting, change of hind leads, roll backs, and three hundred sixty degree turns. These maneuvers just mentioned are expected of the western horse, but are not required of the English horse. Therefore the training methods and the saddles are a lot different. The stirrup leathers on the English saddle are but a double narrow strap, and this permits the rider's legs to rest against the sides of the horse. This contact gives the English horse the advantage of feeling leg pressures a lot easier than that of the western horse. On the western saddle you have a double stirrup leather and the added thickness of the fender between your leg and the sides of the horse.

In my opinion, to get a horse to collect and gather up, more can be accomplished with the cues first given with leg pressure and then followed or enforced by the use of the spur in training. It is a more surefire method than without the spur. The collection process has got to be worked on both ends of the horse. Checking the horse with the hands on the reins, then gathering and collecting with the leg pressure. As this is being done, it is then enforced with the spur or the threat of them to properly train one. I'll get into this more when we are actually riding the horse. I've seen exceptions to what I have written above, but generally I think I am right, and if followed is going to spell success for many of you. The professional English trainers I've known also used the small type English spur in their training.

Sack Hobbles

I have used the burlap sack hobble in my handling of the young horse to a good advantage. This particular kind of hobble to me was very important in the training of the green horse, especially during the earlier riding stage. This helped control the horse while he was getting used to being handled and saddled, bridled, groomed, and many situations that required him to stand still. They are the most humane restraint you can use on the horse. They will not skin or burn a horse which cannot be said of the leather type. However, once a horse has accepted control from the sack hobbles, he then can be hobbled with other types and will not hurt himself.

The horse will resist the hobbles and try to lunge in them when you first put them on, but all the horses I've started after two or three attempts to free their front legs, then would accept the hobbles and would not resist them. Many of you have had the experience of trying to saddle a horse that wants to move ahead or sideways or otherwise make trying to saddle and bridle him an aggravating task. Once a horse is hobble broke, this problem in most cases will stop altogether. It won't be long before you can handle him without them as he has accepted the fact he cannot move. The procedure can be reenacted any time it is required for a refresher course.

I will explain how to make them and tips on how to use them. The burlap material in the feed sack is exceptionally strong. At the same time it is pliable and soft enough to avoid chafing or hurting the horses' front legs. The sack can be obtained at most grain elevators or feed stores throughout the country. A two-bushel sack size is the best, as the one-bushel sack when made up is a little too short. They are not expensive. It might be wise to make up about three or four pair at a time, as sometimes an extra stout horse might draw the square knot so tight that you may have to cut them off. An ordinary pair of pliers will aid in loosening the drawn up knot.

Your first step in making the sack hobble is to open up the sack by unraveling the thread or string that sews one side and the bottom together, as it will be open on the top. If you are unable to unravel the stitches take a pair of scissors and cut down the sides of the thread on the side and bottom of the sack. After having done this, lay the sack on the ground or floor. Be sure to have the sack opened out flat. Take a ruler or yardstick and measure about one foot down from one corner. Mark the measurement with chalk or pencil. Then measure one foot down the other side of the same corner and mark it. Now draw a line across the corner connecting your measuring dots. Cut this corner off with your scissors. Then do exactly the same to the opposite corner of the sack. By cutting these two corners off the sack, it will allow you to roll the remainder of the sack up in a tight compact roll without the hobble being too bulky. Roll the sack up starting at one cut-off portion. Then take a sharp knife and cut a two-inch slot ten inches from the uncut end of the sack. Make sure your knife goes all the way through the layers of burlap. Then after having made the two-inch slit, take the end closest to the cut and run it through the cut. Pull it tight. Do exactly the same on the opposite end. After you have run this opposite end through the cut made, cut one more slot in the center of the hobble and run one end or the other through this center slit. Step on one end and pull hard on the other. This will set your hobbles and they are now complete and ready for use. You have just made a stout pair of hobbles that will sure be hard for any horse to break.

You don't have to worry about getting these hobbles on a horse too tight, because they will stretch enough when a horse tries them that they will be loose enough on him, so they won't hurt him. To put them on you simply put the hobble around both front legs above the fetlock. Measure your two ends, to even them up. Then reach between the horse's front legs from the left side. Make about three or four twists in the hobble between his front legs. Then bring the two ends around his left leg and tie in a square knot. Your horse is now hobbled.

Some may question the use of hobbles on horses as a restraint and a means of control on a green horse. Another method that has been used by old-time bronco men and some modern day trainers is to tie up a hind leg of a horse to get the same effect and control of an animal. But it's been my experience whenever I did I would inevitably burn a horse's fetlock in spite of what type of rope or sling that I used to do it. It would get the job done, but I would have a horse that would be favoring that foot which was tied up, thereby costing me about two weeks or more training on the horse. With some of the older broncy type horses, it was a must. Out of several hundred different horses I've worked, there would not be over twenty-five head that I can remember of having to resort to it. I have never hobbled the hind legs on a horse either. I'm not trying to discredit other trainers or their methods. I'm merely stating the facts pertaining to myself. I also never had or wanted a helper in a breaking pen with me, except on a very few head of horses. I found them either in my way or distracting the attention of the horse that I was trying to work on.

 **5**

Lunging the Horse

Lunging can be an asset in a horse's training if it's done properly, and it won't do him any harm. Some of its advantages are: It will teach the horse a certain amount of collection. It will help him pick up his leads, from a trot to lope, or from a walk to a lope in the correct lead. It will help him adopt a smoother lope or canter. You can also teach him what the word Whoa means. How you do this and where you're doing it makes a big difference in how much easier it will be when you do start riding him. I've found that snuffy or high spirited horses I'm working, that if I put them on a line for about ten to fifteen minutes and worked them both ways before I rode them, they settled down quicker and learned more in a shorter time than if I didn't do it. I would keep any horses that are subject to pitch or buck on a line until they had quit any indication to want to do so prior to each riding session until they had stopped or until I felt that they had enough riding over a period of time to be reasonably sure that they wouldn't blow up. This is especially important when a horse is being box-stalled without being allowed exercise in an area where he can run around or blow off steam.

Some older well-broke horses, can be box-stalled and only ridden three or four times a week and will accept this very well. Where young horses and some cold backed spirited-type horses will react to some degree just the opposite. One thing that should and could be changed at present-day boarding stables is the building and using of some outside exercise paddocks or corrals. If you keep a horse shut up in a box stall and you don't get to ride him for four or five days, especially the colts, you will find them reacting to training much different. Of course, here is another place the lunging of the horse can be an advantage.

The breaking pen or starting corral is the best place to school your horse for this purpose. It's also the place where you can do it alone without help. I won't say it's impossible to lunge a horse in a big enclosure, but you will encounter a lot of problems in doing so. If the horse has been schooled on a line in the small pen and has gotten the knack of it, you can go to a bigger area and be fairly successful in its use. But you might have to have somebody to assist you when you first start the procedure.

We have taken some extra pains in our halter breaking to teach the colt obedience in his leading. We further convinced him with the fifteen-foot rope and loop around his nose that he should, in order not to get his nose pinched, pay attention to that lead rope and the trainer. I strongly suggest that you do not lunge the two-year-old horse you're breaking, or an older one for that matter, in a halter. Use your complete made up hackamore to do it. This will discourage him from attempting to bug out too far on the end of the lunge line. The hackamore will give you a lot of leverage that you cannot obtain from a halter. A horse soon finds out that you can't control him in the halter, and that he can root his nose out and just about get away with anything he wants to do, once he finds out you have a minimum control of his head with the halter. This won't happen if you use the hackamore in lunging him. It will also make it much easier and quicker in your ability to get a turn on him when you start riding him, as he will understand and learn a lot about the hackamore which will be the first piece of equipment used on him when you are starting him. We will now start writing about the actual lunging of the horse.

The only pieces of equipment needed are your complete made-up hackamore and a line about twenty-five feet long. This can be made out of an old used grass rope or sash cord or they have them made up that you can purchase at your western store. You will also need a snap on one end of it. The next and last thing is a lunging whip. They are made up with a long lash with a popper on the end. Let me add here that the whip is not used to really whip the animal but to flick it at him to induce the animal to keep going. It is also used as a signal to go in the opposite direction or stop.

Now assuming you are in the pen where you are going to lunge the horse, and you have the hackamore on the colt. If it's the same one you are going to use on him, when you ride him, attach the snap to one rein. Take the other rein and tie it up on the other side of the horse. You can cut a long slot in the end of the latigo rein where you can loop it over the horn of the saddle, but if he's not saddled slip the opposite rein up under the opposite side of the hackamore head stall. Secure it so it does not fall down. If he's saddled and you loop it around the horn as I have mentioned, make sure there's lots of slack in it, so that the colt has complete head free movement to the inside in the direction he's going. Another way you could go if the horse is saddled would be to have a slot in the ends of both latigo reins and simply loop both over the horn and secure your snap to the bottom of the hackamore.

So now, assuming the hackamore is on the horse with line attached to the hackamore, and if you are starting your horse to the left, get a hold of your line about fifteen feet from your horse. You will have the line in your left hand. The long lashed lunging whip in your right hand. Stand to the side of your horse and this is important, in the early stages of lunging training, don't get ahead of the horse's shoulder on the side that's to you at any time. You may even have to get back further to the rear of the horse to force him forward. Make a movement with your whip hand lightly to the rear of the horse. Remember, don't hit hard; just a flick. You will not have to really bear down with that whip unless he's an exceptionally doggie horse or colt. Use the minimum of discipline to get done with the horse what you're trying to teach him. Increase the discipline only when necessary. Keep your line waist high. Cluck at the horse, flick your whip towards his rear, and once he starts don't use that whip, only when he stops before you say whoa. Keep the horse moving around you at a trot for the first two or three sessions. Do not change and go the other direction until the horse is doing and going well in the direction that your first attempts were made. Remember, flick the whip only enough at and on him to get him to trot.

At first you will be making a big circle behind the shoulder of the horse. Once he's starting to respond, you can shorten the inside circle you're making and give the horse more line. If your pen is square, he will try to hang up in the corners. So think ahead of him, as with all horses in training. Give a pull on that line just before he gets to the corner. Then a flick of that whip to get him by it. It won't be long before he will stop trying to stop in those corners. Once this is accomplished, you are ready to think about how you are going to get this horse schooled to stop on command.

Drop your whip to the ground out of your hand. Start out towards the front of your horse. Raise your arms and say "whoa" loud and clear. He will stop. Let the horse remain there. Do not pull him in to you. Go to him, and pet him and talk a little saying, "Good, good." The tone of voice should be soothing and just loud enough where he can hear it. Move back towards the end of your line, but try to make the horse stand where he's at. You may have to step in front of him again and raise your arms and say "whoa" again sharp and clear. Another thing I will mention here is that extra line you will be having. Here are the don'ts: Don't take a rap around your hand. Watch the slack that's on the ground. As you move around in the small circle you're making facing the horse, you will have to step over that excess line. Do not let this horse go around you letting raps being taken around either one of your legs or both. If you would get in a storm and lose control of the horse, he could upset you and drag you.

Let us say after a few lessons, we have progressed to the point where the horse is trotting around you fairly smooth, and he has stopped trying to stop in those corners. When you're out in the middle of your pen and the horse is starting to stop and remain in position by seeing you drop the whip, and the fact that you move a little to the front of him at the same time you're giving him the command "whoa," he will soon take the signal. When you drop the whip, he's expected to stop and on the command "whoa" should do so.

At this point you will stop going to the horse to reward him. Stay away from him. His reward will be that he gets a brief rest on each stop. Use the voice reward "good" about twice.

From this point on, if for any reason you go to the horse, drop your line and whip before going to him. Also, when you are ready to quit the lesson, drop your lunge line and whip. Walk to him. Disengage the line and leave it lay there. You can coil it up later. Get your lead rope and halter to put on the horse after removing the hackamore.

Let us assume that your horse is now circling to the left at a trot. You have changed your position to the end of the line and you are turning as the horse turns almost in one spot. The horse is stopping on cue. He is ready to start to lope on the line. Let and expect him to be urged into this lope from a trot. Once he has made a couple of circles around you fairly well, it won't be perfect at first, stop him in the same way we described and reward with the words "good boy." One reason I forgot to mention in my previous description of why I'd go to the horse instead of pulling him into the circle, is to encourage him to stay there until the sessions are completed. By pulling the horse in to you at any time, he's liable to come to you when he thinks he wants to quit. By repetition of dropping this whip, and you are saying the word "whoa" as you do it, and having stopped the horse by moving slightly towards the front of him, the horse has observed your actions. He will soon learn to do it while you are in the middle of the circle, and you will not have to be stopping him by going ahead of his shoulder. Let me say again, watch your position. Don't get, or let the horse get you, in the position where you're not just a little behind his shoulder, as this will encourage him to want to check or stop.

The next procedure you will undertake is to start the horse in the opposite direction. But make sure he is progressing pretty fair to the left before you change and start schooling to the right. When you have this done, and he's working both ways fairly well, he will soon be thinking and doing the following things: When you stop him, it will be on the voice command "whoa." When you change your line from your left hand to your right hand and put the whip in you left hand, he will soon know which way he's expected to go when you make these moves. It won't be long before when he sees you change the line and whip to the opposite hand, you can say whoa and he will stop. When you change the line and whip to the other hand, take one step ahead of him, hold your line higher. He will then turn in his tracks and head the other way. Study what's been written here. Remember it and you will be able to understand and apply it. I have applied the same procedure successfully on many different horses. While a trainer will do most of these things automatically and make faster time with the horse, the novice will have to think out everything he's going to do. It also takes a good deal more time for the unskilled to accomplish it. But refer back to what I've written. Study mistakes you might be making, and you will come out okay.

I never was much on walking a horse on a line. It was always for only two purposes: (1) To lunge him prior to riding him. To let him take out the kinks if he was high. (2) To exercise him. If you teach him to lunge properly you'll have a better horse for it. Anything a person can do to make and further his mount, he will get more fun and rewards from the handling of his horse. I'll add again "patience" is a must. Never punish a horse physically unless you're very sure he goofed on purpose and that he knows better. Again

I'm going to stress that the persons that are attempting to do their own training should take time in doing it. When you have seen a degree of improvement in the horse you are trying to teach, stop for that session while you are ahead. This will allow the horse some satisfaction that he has gotten along with you, and he won't learn to hate the training sessions. If his mind is fresh, he will try harder than when he's weary of it.

My lunging experience was always used in connection with the horses I was riding. Especially the first saddlings. But it will work in either instance, saddled or unsaddled. I might add here that the lunging of the saddled green horse prior to his riding took the place of driving him for me.

I have never driven a horse that I was starting. From the time he hit my training stable, I'd be on him either the second or third day I had him. I'd not stay up on him very long, just long enough for him to get acquainted with the fact that I was up there. I could never quite believe that I couldn't do more with my hands close to the animal's head than if I were behind him, with a fifteen-foot pair of lines trying to drive him. Anyway, I knew I would have to get on him sooner or later. I think I made faster progress by doing it sooner.

In reviewing the lunging process we have just covered, I had forgotten to bring some points about starting this horse from a walk into his proper right or left lead in a lope. After you have him traveling around you both ways in a lope, it's quite simple. As you have already put the stop on him from voice command, and also the changing of the line and whip from one hand to the other. Watch the horse closely as he starts to gallop. The hind leg nearest you will be under him further than his outside leg. This is his correct lead. If you don't see this correct hind leg position, stop him and start over. You may have to go back and start in a trot again until he picks it up. You will find that horses for the most part are right or left lead horses. The one he uses the most will be his true lead. You seldom have trouble with that one. It will be the off lead which is not his favorite that will give you the most trouble to accomplish. But hang in there, you can do it.

 6

Preliminaries Prior to Riding

Most horses at present are starting their actual riding training at age two. Of course, there are many hours of time spent on most horses when they are a good deal younger such as handling, halter breaking, and manners. These are all necessary before his actual riding training starts. They are also a must for novice riders before they attempt to ride a green horse.

So let me describe what I think to be an ideal young horse to start riding. (1) I would have the horse well halter broke; (2) a horse that has had his feet handled; (3) a horse that has been handled enough so that it is not jumpy; (4) a horse that is in good health; (5) a horse that is sound, at least where his conformation is good enough to carry some weight without breaking down; (6) he should be at least a full two years old. There is a saying if he's big enough he's old enough. I don't go along with the statement. Of course, there are exceptions such as horses being prepared for the race track. These horses are for the most part ridden with English saddles and lightweight riders on their back. There is probably a difference of eighty pounds. Also the fact that they have to be pushed harder in training to get them ready to run in their second year. Some day I think they will stop racing the quarter horse at age two. This I would heartily approve. I think they are too young for the strain that's put on them at this age.

I would like a horse's weight to be in the thousand-pound weight class. One thousand pounds or heavier weight fine, but eight hundred to nine hundred acceptable. A lot of quarter horses and Arabs will not weigh this much before they are a full two and some not then. I'm trying to point out that it's not a good policy to ride horses too small at too early of an age. They are more difficult to train. What happens to trainers and those who try to school the too small or too young animal is they find that they run into a lot of difficulties. These small horses have a tendency to funnel out on their front quarters, making it difficult and sometimes impossible to keep a saddle in position on their backs. This is especially true of so many young horses that are round withered. Most of the time they grow out of this as they get older and mature out. You have to cinch the young horse tight enough to hold the saddle in place. When you do this on the round withered colt, it's probably too tight for comfort. This alone is enough to make him rebel, try to buck, sometimes rear up, and even throw himself out of sheer aggravation.

I think this to be a direct cause of cinch bound horses. They start a bad habit which sometimes they carry, to some degree, all their life. While your saddle is working ahead on the colt, the cinch rings are forced into his shoulder muscles. This is more true of horses with too straight of a shoulder and round withers. You seldom have this problem in horses with a long slope to their shoulders. This is one reason I've liked the strong thoroughbred-type quarter horse to train. Most of them have the long shoulder necessary to produce the good saddle back. The cinch ring will set well back from the shoulder muscle.

Now we will take the too small, round withered funneled out to the front variety colt and start out on a training session. We find that going straight he doesn't go too badly, but we can't go straight forever. We have got to start bending him sooner or later, whether it be in a snaffle bit or a hackamore. Now we find the horse reluctant to turn on the side pull or plow rein. So we pull harder. If he knew enough to move his shoulder over away from the cinch ring, he would avoid the pain being inflicted by the cinch ring. But he doesn't, and he won't for some time as this occurs later on in his training. What does happen, however, is he gives with his head and neck, and because he doesn't know enough to move his front leg and shoulder over with his head and neck, thus moving his shoulder away from the cinch ring pressure, pain is inflicted. He then rebels and does not want to give you his head at all. If he's allowed to get away with this, you are on the way to having a spoiled horse. He is liable to find out that if he tries to run he can get his head, or if he rears up the pain stops. If he can find a way that works for him to relieve the discomfort even for a minute he will take it. In other words, he has a training session going for him to thwart my efforts to train him. It also takes some thinking and study on the rider's part to overcome this.

Horse with long sloped shoulder and good withers

Photography by Neil Mishler, Ponca, Nebraska

If a horse is not well halter broke, he's going to be difficult to saddle. So have the horse good halter broke before you start to ride him. While you're halter breaking him, tie him up enough so he isn't pulling back every time you raise your arm or move around him. We can get around a lot of this by using a sack hobble. There is probably nothing that aggravates a person more than to have a horse jump ahead or sideways when you try to saddle him. The best way is to make him want to stand still. To get that across to him is to force him to stand. I know of no other faster or surefire method to do it than to hobble break him.

Now let us get to the disposition of the horse. A careful study of the colt will reveal a lot about his nature. If he's a doggie raised colt and accepts everything you do with him without jumping when you groom him, and will allow you to handle him on both sides, and pick up his feet, this horse presents, at least in his early stages of riding, far less difficulty than the jumpy nervous-type colt. If he is in the nervous jumpy category, you will have to work slower and take more pains with him than you do the doggie colt. In other words, if your horse is not ready to start riding training and rather than to take chances on pushing him too rapidly, I suggest you work with him more on the ground until he's reached the point where the ground work is not improving him further.

Horse training is basically taking a step at a time with the animal. From the time a colt is foaled until the day you first put your hands on him, he is more or less under the influence of his mother and nature. But when human hands are placed on him, he's being schooled from that point on by his association with man. So what we do with him, and more important is how we do it, has and will play a big part in how he turns out later on.

After a colt goes through the stages of halter breaking and handling up to the actual riding training, the methods you use will help a lot to his becoming a well mannered colt later on when his riding starts. There are some do's and don'ts in the preliminary stages as there are in the advanced schooling.

Sacking out is an old expression. This is a method that was widely used by early day horse breakers on range horses and mustangs. These kind of horses in the case of mustangs had never had a hand on them. The domestic-type range horse, only when branded and castrated. They seldom knew man except from a distance or on the round-up. So they were not too much different from the mustang as far as handling was concerned. When they were picked out for the rough string man to break, they were hardly ever broke before age three and up. Once corraled, he would be put into a breaking pen, front footed, haltered, tied up, and sometimes ridden before he would lead. He'd have a hind leg jacked up, wooled around, and he would then be sacked out. Feed sacks were lightweight and were not expensive. They were flapped around every part of the horse's body, along perhaps with a pair of chaps, sometimes tied on the end of a short rope, then dabbed at the horse from every direction. I never liked to sack a horse's head. I don't think it should be done, but have seen some men do it. The horse would also have a pair of sack or rope hobbles on his front legs. He was a stout, wild as a deer, unhandled, fully matured horse, and sometimes fat, with a lot of fight in him as only this kind of horse could have. So faced with these facts, and that they had an immediate use for the horses, prompted trainers of that period to take every shortcut that would make a broke horse out of the animal as soon as possible. Their methods worked, but it took a certain breed of men to get along with them after they were broke. The picture has changed. There are more horses used as hobbies than necessities today. The methods have changed now to fit the kind of riders that ride them today. Also by studying the horses more trainers are taking more time to produce a gentle capable horse that average people can get along with and enjoy.

The sacking way to gentle a spooky horse is okay, providing it's done right. One thing is important. Don't overdo it. You can instill a bug or quirk in a horse if you aren't careful.

If I were a novice trainer or owner intending to advance my own horse, I would not do the following: If my horse is coming along and getting more gentle by other means and was handling fairly well, I'd not sack him at all. In any event don't hit your colt on the head to punish him, nor sack him around his ears or head. This sensitive area is the cause of a lot of head-shy horses. It raises his suspicions about any movement in that area leading to a fear of being haltered or bridled later on. To avoid this, be careful when working or handling around a horse's head and ears.

There are more bugs and quirks instilled in horses during these early handling stages by the people that handle them than any natural way a horse might pick them up. Extreme care must be taken to avoid them. Some things can happen by accident that can't be helped but handlers can do a lot to prevent most of them. For example, a rider that is used to a single cinch on his saddle and not a double cinch will forget to undo his rear girth first, but undo the front cinch. When he starts to pull the saddle from the horse, and if the horse is a jumpy bronc-type horse, disaster will follow. It is not likely the horse will tolerate what's happening. He will start to lunge and kick, and if you cannot reach that back billet right away to loosen this saddle, he will damage it and possibly demolish it. The horse after going through this experience will remember it for a long, long time. This could cause him to react to any movement or object that reminded him of the experience. Thus instilling a bug in the horse.

I've never heard a satisfactory explanation as to why some horses shy more than others. Some get over it and some never do. One of the reasons given or heard is his vision. I can't buy it. I think something happened, and we are talking about the chronic shying horse, that left an imprint on this horse's mind that he cannot forget. It would not have to be man-made. But sometimes it is. I've worked on some horses that had bad cases of it. Although I made some progress with them, I was never fully satisfied with the results. I failed to find a complete answer to the problem.

Starting the Green Colt

I think what started me to finally getting around to using different procedures in starting and training the horses I was working was the fact that there was getting to be a big demand for horses that would go into western pleasure classes at horse shows. Prior to that time, I did not pay too much attention to head position, leads and cues for leads, or what a horse would have to do to win this particular event. After going to horse shows and watching some of these classes and seeing how good they were made me realize that I was going to have to do some things I had not been doing before towards that end. I'd more or less just break these horses and put a slow neck rein on them, so I could lope them out. They would usually take a few steps backwards and in general, be just a horse to ride, which is about all the average horse ridden for pleasure or hobby was required to do.

Then the demand for these horses that would go into pleasure competition started to assert itself. More people wanted to participate, and they were not experts in their capabilities to ride horses in any other competition. I told myself I was going to have to change my methods to satisfy this market in my training program. After about two years of pretty steady progress in this direction, the demand for reining horses also increased. I found out that everything I did with the training of the pleasure horse for competition also gave me some big advantages in producing the reining horse later on. So I started to school my competition horses with this thought in mind. If the person owning the horse that I was training for pleasure wanted to rein the horse later, I would get the same horse back for reining training and other competition events the following year. I also learned that the pleasure training using my methods would result in the same horse, if inclined in that direction, to be much easier to train in other events, roping cutting, barrels, or you name it. I would receive horses for advanced training that I had not broke or formally trained. In the process of training them, it made me realize the mistakes the previous owners and trainers had made when they started them. In winding up this phase of the writing, I'll say I have proved to myself that horses schooled with my methods will be successful. A lot depends on how he was started from the time he was first saddled and thereafter. Some of these ideas may be questioned, but if they are followed, they will succeed.

So let us start with a full two-year-old colt or filly and go into our breaking pen or corral. Let us say we have one post that we are going to use for a tie post or snubbing post. In the old days this post would be placed in the center of the pen and would be stuck in the ground four feet deep. I have seen some of these old posts that had one to two-inch rope indentations on them, which was the result of having a lot of stock snubbed to them. It is not advisable in this day and age to put the tie post in the center. I would place it next to the fence, but on the inside of the fence or corral just the opposite of the rest of the posts supporting the pen. I would choose a ten-foot long post and eight inches in diameter. Sink it four feet in the ground. I would do a good job of tamping that post also. It will be on the inside of the pen. All other posts in your corral if you were to build one would be on the outside, with planks or whatever material used on the inside. The tie post, if placed on the outside of the breaking pen would, when a horse set or pulled back on his halter, pull against the fence causing the fence to come out of line. There will be some give to the post if pulled back on by a stout horse. There's a good reason for the rest of the posts to be placed on the outside of the pen. When you lunge your horse, your stirrups will not be hanging up on the posts as your horse circles. More important is the fact that I've had both knees injured on those posts put on the inside. You can get by with just the snubbing post on the inside, but if you have a row of them around you, you'll hit one sooner or later with your foot or leg. Several planks nailed on the inside of these posts would prevent injury or prevent your hanging a leg or boot on one of them.

On this snubbing post, I like to take a heavy piece of rope, one I know a stout horse can't break. Then buy a big snap at the western store or hardware store, one that I know even a tough horse can't break. I like to tie this lead rope in a permanent position on this post high enough which would be about one foot above the withers of a fifteen and one-half-hand high horse. It will then work for all horses tied to it. I like to lead the horse I'm going to ride up to the post and snap the stout tie rope on the post to the halter. Leave the light lead rope on the halter. You will use it while putting the hackamore or snaffle head stall on your horse. It will also be used again when I put the horse away. I don't want this horse we are going to ride to pull back on the lead rope and break it. It will happen on an average size lead rope. If it's nylon, he won't break the rope, but when he pulls back will probably break the snap if you don't use a stout one.

The horse hobbled with sack hobbles
Photography by Nell Mishler, Ponca, Nebraska

If the horse's halter is questionable as to strength, put one on that is stout. Put it on him before tying him to the snub post.

Let us say that the first thing you will do in this first session is to introduce your horse to the sack hobbles. We will not tie the horse to the snub post for these first sack hobble sessions. Take two pair of sack hobbles into the pen with you. Place one on the fence. Then hobble your horse with the other. Once hobbled remove your lead rope. Leave your halter on. Step away from him and just stand and wait. Let him try these hobbles for several minutes. It won't be long before he will decide to stand still. Don't try to stop him. If he manages to get out of them, recatch him. Get the pair off the fence and put them on him. This time draw them up tighter by twisting closer in the middle and pull your square knot tighter on the left side. Let him loose again. The reason for taking the lead rope off is he will sometimes, in his efforts to free himself, get that lead rope tangled up in his hobble. Avoid this. Take the lead rope off for this session. When he has given up, work with him on the ground, groom him, and pet him on all sides. Once he has quit resisting the hobble and is standing still, quit for that session.

The main reason for turning this horse loose with the hobble rather than standing there with the lead rope in your hand is that if he moves ahead, trying the hobble, he is liable to lash out with both front feet in his efforts to get them off. If you move back away from him, he's liable to get the idea he is being led and will go further ahead in the hobbles than he would if he were loose and you're not near him. We want him to learn that once hobbled it is not associated with the trainer. We will at no time pull ahead or sideways on the lead rope on the horse while he is hobbled.

The reason I do not tie this horse up the first few saddlings is due to the fact he's hobbled. After he has been hobbled several sessions, and if he's giving you trouble, you can tie him first, then hobble him and it will work okay. But I've found that tying him up on the first few saddlings and hobbling him as well could result in his throwing himself due to the fact he is not hobble broke. He won't do this when he's tied once he's had hobble experience.

On the first session prior to saddling, we introduced the colt to the hobbles and left them on long enough to convince the horse it's difficult for him to move in them. In his efforts to free himself it was put across to him that he couldn't get it done. On this first saddling session after you have him in the starting corral, put your sack hobbles on him. Then step back. Watch him. If he fails to test the hobbles, push a little on his shoulder to force him to try them. Just enough so he knews he is hobbled. Then put your hackamore on him in place of the halter. Don't have any loose equipment lying around the corral while working your horse.

Go back out of the pen and get your saddle. Before you saddle the horse remove the rear girth. You might also take the back rear billet off on the right side. In this way you will not have so much interference with equipment that you aren't going to use. Because on this first saddling anything that can help you get the horse saddled will be an improvement in the process. Take a guess how the adjustment might have to be on the billet holding the front cinch. Sometimes you get pretty accurate at this. After having done the above, pick your saddle up. You won't need a blanket this first time out. All you're going to do is saddle the horse, not ride him. Make sure that your latigo is run through your rigging ring so that you will not be stepping on it when you place the saddle on the horse. Take your saddle into the pen. Approach your hobbled horse from the front, going in and towards the horse at an angle from the front as though you were going towards his shoulder on the left side. Go in slowly. When you are close enough to him let him smell and examine it while you're still holding it. Then walk around the horse within three or four feet from him about three or four times in each direction carrying the saddle. Then go in again towards him, let him smell of it again. Lay it down about three feet in front of his front legs. Then step back and let him look and smell of it until he has examined it thoroughly.

Now pick up your saddle. Go around where you're just ahead of his shoulder on the left side. Lay it down about two feet to one side of the horse. Reach down and get the hackamore reins and place the end of them in your left hip pocket. Do it quietly. Don't move in jerks in all the following actions. Then reach down slowly and pick up your right stirrup. At the same time place the end of the cinch in the same hand that you have the stirrup in. Take your right hand and put your fingers through the gullet from the top. Raise the saddle and place the cinch and stirrup gently over his back. Then release the cinch and stirrup. Put that hand on the front of the saddle. Take your right hand from the gullet and get hold of the cantle of your saddle. Let it slowly down on the horse's back. Be as careful as you can. If the horse jumps out at this time, simply grasp your saddle and step back. Grab the reins with your left hand to check him until he's stopped and start the procedure over. It's possible that he will move out but not likely. If he does move out replace your saddle where you think it should set on him. Pat the horse a little. Speak to him encouragingly using the words "good boy" or "fine." Then go around to the right side. Look at your billet and cinch. Check them making sure that they are positioned right. Go back to the left-hand side. Take your left stirrup and hang it on the saddle horn. Right here it gets a little sticky. You reach down and get this cinch with your right hand. Keep your eye on your horse's eye and ears. He will usually let you know if he's going to make a move. I'm going to suggest here that if you were attempting to saddle a horse that might be inclined to wheel and kick or what I call cow-kick at you, when you reach under the horse. It is at this point, if he's going to kick, that he might do it. If you're not sure of the horse, simply take a piece of number nine wire about a yard long, and fashion a small hook on one end of the wire. Use it to hook the cinch ring to bring it up to your hand. Now raise up on this cinch resting it very lightly against the hair. Then take a look to see if the cinch is centered on the horse. You want the middle of the cinch to be in the center of the horse. If it looks okay, have the reins in your hip pocket. Reach down, get the cinch again with your right hand. Watch your horse's head occasionally. Pick up your latigo. Run it through your rigging ring and cinch with two wraps. Make sure at this point your cinch is not resting against the hide of your horse. The wraps should be loose. This done, take your right hand and hold the cinch so that it's just touching your horse's hide as you did at first letting him feel it. Take your left hand and work your latigo tight a little at a time until it's about taken the slack out between where you have been holding it against him with your left hand. Now take both hands and very gently take up on your latigo. Do a quarter of an inch at a time until it's snug. Keep watching your horse's eyes and ears. Now we have the slack out and your cinch is resting fairly snug on the horse, but it is still not quite tight enough to hold this saddle in place, when we turn him loose with the empty rig on. At this point take up about one more hole. If we were to ride this horse at this time, we would really have to cinch him much tighter. So we will work it tight enough so that the saddle won't turn and that's all. It will take about one more hole up in the latigo. You can tell by just putting your fingers under the latigo. If you have to push a little to get them under there, you are tight enough. If not, take up another hole. If you have worked easy and taken your time, this horse should not have moved out.

Remove the left stirrup from the horn to the down position. Now you have him saddled. Tie your hackamore reins fairly loose to the saddle horn. Reach down and free his legs from the hobbles and step back. The horse may stand for a brief period or he may move out right away. If he doesn't, take your sack hobble and shake it at him. Make him move. Before we describe what he is going to do, I'm going to write my ideas why I have used the methods that I have. Most colts will make some kind of an attempt to pitch in their early riding. The common expression, "Hold his head up," is heard from a lot of people. This may work for you later on when you are riding the horse, but at this time you can determine a lot of things from watching this horse on his first two saddlings when loose in this pen with the empty saddle on. They are as follows: You can tell how hard he can buck. How long he bucks. Whether he has little or a big interest in bucking at all. Shall we say when he first moves out with that empty rig, if he squalls and really hits it and keeps at it for about three rounds around this pen, he has shown us that he is capable of pitching, and that he kind of likes and wants to do it. So we will watch this horse a little closer in the future than the horse that takes two or three hops and quits. If he is in that category take your sack hobble and keep moving him around in the pen for awhile. A little of it won't hurt the other kind either. When he has quit bucking and humping, go to him, untie your reins from the saddle horn, and lead him around for about ten minutes. Then take your hobble and re-hobble him. Pat him a lot. Reward him with "good boy," "good boy," and remove your saddle. Put him away. We will go further in his next lesson.

Up to this point we have hobble broke a horse, have saddled him and have determined how tough to ride he might be. We will repeat this again today. Only we will lunge the horse with the saddle on. We will also put the back cinch on the saddle and use a saddle blanket under the saddle. You tighten the back cinch up just so that it rests lightly against his hide, because while loose in the pen with the empty rig, he will adjust to the feel of the rear girth. You can expect some reaction to it with a horse that's inclined to want to buck.

I've been asked many times, which I refer to as strictly a dude question, it is: "Do I buck the horses out that I train?" So here is my answer: I don't encourage it. I don't want him to, but knowing that he may do it at the beginning or later when he's under training pressure, I like to find out early just how tough he is. You can get a pretty good idea from watching those first two saddlings and also on the lunge line later just what he is inclined to want to do. You can't keep stealing a ride on horses and train them. Number one is to stay on your horse. So I'd rather he did his worst with that empty saddle and not win than taking chances later when I'm on him when he's never tried it. Most all horses I've started do not buck but little. The ones that did, I always tried to be ready for them. One thing that has helped carry me through many storms, and I am sure I would have got bucked off but for it, was a wide leather strap that I carried through the fork of my saddle. Being right-handed I would place this strap to the right of my saddle horn. It would be adjusted so that it was pretty hard to miss it. If I was in a position with a rein in each hand, and a horse started to really buck, I would make a quick transfer of my right rein to my left hand. I'd make a pass at that strap, keeping my spurs out of the horse, and ninety-nine percent of the time I'd make it.

I first saw the use of this strap in East Oregon on horse round-ups. They also tied their right stirrup to the center of their cinch so they would make sure that they did not have to fish for the right stirrup on a broncy horse. The hackamore men would take the McCarty and instead of tying it neatly to the left side of the saddle, would tuck this into their jacket. In case they got unloaded, they would grab for it and have one more chance at not having to make a long walk through sagebrush to camp or ranch.

When I stated that ninety percent of the horses I started did not buck at all, I'll rephrase that to after the first week. The point I'm trying to get across is that most two-year-olds won't take over two or three hops. Which you really could not call bucking. Most anybody could ride them. But as I never turned down any horses as long as I got paid to ride them, I did run into about every kind of horse there is in this country. This is why I feel qualified to write this book. I rode horses for fifteen years straight for a living. I had no other job for my income. Going back I had an opportunity to work with and observe some pretty good hands with training horses. I learned a lot from them in my youth, and I am grateful to them for it. I would like to put in here, I've taken some hard knocks in this business. I think to be a good trainer can be summed up in this way: Each horse is an individual. They are generally alike, but each one has or develops his own hangups. My opinion is that if a horse is not responding to a given procedure in one phase or another that has worked on other horses, the trainer has got to know horses well enough to come up with something new for that particular horse. The man or woman who can do this has my respect and admiration.

Let me say that the instructions here have been presented to you by a trainer who has had a lot of stock to try them out on. Through the years I tried to choose the most effective methods that got the job done, and I continued to use them. If you have the time you can vary them. For instance you could lunge the colt for a couple of weeks with your saddle on prior to riding. On the second week of lunging you could also take two sacks full of hay and tie them shut at the top. Then take a piece of rope long enough to tie them together. Hobble and tie your horse. Then put a sack on each side of your saddle horn. Take a couple of half hitches around your horn with this connecting rope. Tie one corner of the stuffed sack to each stirrup. This would cause the horse to have less fear of your body movements when mounted. You might also take a pair of chaps and lay each leg over the rump of the horse and tie each leg to a saddle string on each side of the saddle behind the cantle. After a few sessions on the lunge line the colt would be less tempted to spook when you first mount him, lessening the chances of your losing control of him at that point. It would serve as a form of sacking out while the horse is in motion.

We have also taken off the back cinch preparatory to saddling him for the first time. We do this so that we would have less complications handling the saddle and also have caused the horse less aggravation and fear by doing so. We replaced it later before riding him.

I have read some books on training. These books would take one-half of the volume to cover different breeds of horses and names of different events, but the titles of the books would be such that a person buying one would find that rather than reading something useful in the teaching of his horse, would be buying instead all that extra literature about statistics of the horse. Which is probably interesting, but not on instructions as he thought would be in them. I'm trying to get training across to you. If I stray from a subject, it will still be related to training and have a purpose.

I've tried to cross-tie skittish colts to groom them and saddle them. It didn't work well, for me, but I found out I could hobble one, and it wouldn't take the horse long to understand that I had sure made it hard for him to get away with too much. It is amazing what this does to a horse. It will definitely change his mind that he can't be handled. By instilling this in his mind, you have opened the door to his respect. From this point on, common sense and by not hurting him, he will not blame you for the hobbles or saddle on his back, if you're careful to always be a little kind and gentle in your other handling and personal contact.

I am less afraid of a wild horse biting me than some gentle old stud that might do it when my back is to him when I'm leading him. I am also less afraid of the young stud I'm starting to ride, than I am of the older gentle more trusted kind. I've started many young studs and have really never run into a real mean one yet. I like them. I got along with them good and most of them turned out well, as well as a lot of geldings or mares. But you have to watch them a little closer because they have sex on their mind a lot of the time instead of what you're trying to teach them.

Another thing I won't do that I've heard some people advise others to do in the handling of two-year-olds and up, they advocate getting on them in a box stall. I strongly advise you, don't try getting on a green horse in a box stall. I would rather see you walking than visit you in a hospital.

One trainer said that the hackamore was a very crude piece of equipment compared to the snaffle bit. He never got acquainted with the hackamore's use too much. He probably had a bad experience with a runaway colt in traffic or lost control of his horse and got bucked off from an English saddle while out in the open.

I worked a lot of horses that had never seen a box stall. The first thing I'd do was to teach them to face out to me when I went in to take them out of the stall. The broncy ones that were halter broke I'd try the grain approach to make them face out. If this didn't work, I'd step inside, close the door and threaten him a little to bring him out of the far corner. Then let him stand. I'd approach him again and repeat it if he withdrew back and stuck his head in the corner. Something else that worked pretty well was a long stick about six feet long with a piece of number nine wire fashioned with a short hook on the end. Staple the wire to the stick with small staples or tape to secure it. Reach out slow with it and hook the halter ring when he's half facing out to you. It will work, but it might take a few days, before he will face out to you on his own.

Many people outside or in will walk up to a horse from the rear to catch him. If you're sure of the horse and know him, okay, but if he's new to you don't do it.

One other thing I'll point out to you. If possible catch your horse in a box stall leaving the door open behind you all the way. Try it, but if you do close the door behind you, do not go far enough into the stall that you reverse your position with the horse. Where you are trapped on the far end and he is in the corner at the door, because if you try to get back to the door, you could get kicked or knocked down when he goes by as you try to get back to the door.

While we are on the subject of stalls, the right way to put a horse away or back in the stall is to go in the stall leading the horse. Go back far enough so you can make a complete turn. Then go back to the door, and with the horse facing you unsnap him. I leave halters on my horses in the stalls. In case of fire I can lead him out. Care must be taken that objects are not in the stall that he might hang up on especially self-watering cups or hooks or nails.

If you turn a horse loose in a paddock or exercise pen, go through the gate and make a complete turn as you did in your box stall. Make your horse face you. Don't turn him loose right away, wait maybe ten seconds, then release him. Don't go into that paddock and turn the horse loose on the way into the pen. Because if you do and he's high and feeling good, even gentle horses will sometimes jump up in the air and kick high behind. I got kicked on the elbow one time by a shod horse. I kind of woke up after that. I also had an apprentice trainer working for me a few years later. He was leading a perfectly gentle Arab gelding. He turned this gelding loose the wrong way. The horse was turned loose, and just as he was passing by the handler, he playfully kicked high behind kicking this boy in the jaw breaking it. The horse being shod, the end of the shoe went clear through his cheek. He's okay now. I thought this might be worth warning you about.

I don't believe you can put the young horse in a snaffle bit at the very beginning of his training and drive him in the snaffle with a long set of reins without pulling too hard on them, without starting to toughen up his mouth. So I'm going to say if you drive him do it in the hackamore. The worst thing you could do is to tie a horse's head around with a snaffle bit. You are bound to injure and hurt his mouth with it. Some of the old trainers of many years back would do this, and they may still do it. But don't you do it. Use your hackamore for this job of limbering up his neck.

As for leverage steel shanked, mechanical hackamores. The only thing they are good for is in a situation where you have a horse that has no mouth left, but is broke and neck reins fairly well. He may work in the mechanical hackamore, but it is a piece of equipment that's sure useless in training a green horse. If a person uses it on them, he's making a mistake. You see them on dogging and roping horses quite a bit. So they must have some value there. But as to my opinion, these same horses were not put in the mechanical hackamore only after their mouth went bad. Some ropers have a habit of leaving their horse riding their rein. That might account for the horse being in the mechanical hackamore. I could never quite understand it on the dogging horse, as he doesn't have to stop. But not being a bull dogger will not engage further in that direction. I was a calf roper for many years. I always wanted a bit on a horse, nor did I ever resort to some long-shanked freak bit either. For any speed event horse, to make him right is to do the things I'm putting in this book. You can't just take a horse and go out there and bat and spur your way to an all-around horse. Some place along the line you are going to have to take some time, judgement, and a lot of hours and sessions of training to accomplish it using the right methods.

 8

First Rides on Greenie

After having hobbled the colt for the first time, and he has accepted them along with his first saddling experience that he's had, we watched him closely to determine how much he resisted the saddle on his back. How hard he bucked, if any, or whether he just trotted off with a little hump in his back. The latter is what most colts that have had a lot of handling by their owners will do. The colts that have been handled less are the ones that put up the most resistance to the trainer's or handler's efforts in starting them under saddle. After having made these observations we can get a pretty clear-cut idea as to how fast we can take the horse in his early training. If he's the gentle much handled type, we can assume he will train faster as a beginner, more so, than the more frisky less handled type colt. But after the first two weeks' work it could be just the opposite.

On the first two saddlings these colts should be left saddled for perhaps forty-five minutes to one hour each session. They should also be worked with on the ground. It helps to move the stirrup leathers by hand backward and forward on the sides of the animal. This should be done while the horse is hobbled. The stirrup leathers can also be slapped gently on the sides of the horse to acquaint him with them. This will then not alarm him so much when you mount him, and he sees and feels your leg movements for the first time. It also might be advisable at different periods to catch him in the pen, and loosen and retighten the cinch tight enough to where the saddle would stay on him when the time comes to ride him for the first time. This will help him get used to the feel of the cinch quicker also.

After having lunged the horse for about fifteen minutes, and although he is sloppy in his movements around you, you have also had the opportunity to watch him and form an opinion of his actions while putting a little pressure on him in that process. If he's had previous lunging experience prior to saddling, he will go right back into the routine after a very short time while saddled. However, if he has not had lunging experience both the saddling and lunging lessons can go on at the same time causing no harm.

On the second saddling and thereafter, you will use blankets on the horse. You should use enough blanket to make sure there's a good cushion between the saddle and the back of your horse. If you use a too thin blanket, it will induce him to react unfavorably to the saddle pressure. Too much or many blankets will make you have to cinch the horse up tighter than it would be necessary to allow comfort to his back. These things must be considered by the trainer to get the best results. The equipment is strange to the horse in its early usage. All things that are uncomfortable to him in regard to his reactions will add to his anxieties about them.

On the second saddling, we will continue to put a hackamore on the horse in place of the halter. This will be done after you have hobbled the horse's front legs. Don't lunge your horse in the halter. Do it after you put your hackamore on him. As referred to before, the latigo reins on your hackamore are going to be used to a good advantage from here on out.

Now this horse has been saddled twice and won't do much when you place that blanket or blankets gently down on his back. We will also change our method a little when we put our saddle on him. We now have put the back cinch and billet back on the

(a) Position of hands on saddle on the first saddling of the hobbled horse; (b) Easing saddle on hobbled horse

Photography by Neil Mishler, Ponca, Nebraska

saddle. So take both cinches and your stirrup leather and stirrups on the right side and place them over the seat of your saddle. These are now out of the way. Place a hand on each end of the saddle and lower it gently and slowly down in position on the horse's back. Go around to the right side and slowly bring your stirrups and cinches down and position each where it belongs. Go back around to the left side. Put both of those hackamore reins in your left hip pocket. Reach down and get your front cinch and cinch it up as tight as you did on your first two saddlings. Then adjust your back one. We will cinch this horse tighter after we have lunged him and prior to mounting the first time. Loop your latigo reins with a slot in each end around the horn of the saddle. Take off your hobbles, and let him move around on his own for about five minutes. Now if this colt has had lunging training, you should not have any difficulty starting him in this procedure. He will react a little different because he's saddled and still getting used to it. However, if he has not had the lunging experience, you can start it now. But for the first week, we will only go with him to the left as most of them work that way better. We will stay with this left lead lunging until we have the horse loping in that direction which would probably take about a week's lunging. Our main reason for the lunging at this point is to take the edge off the horse. After lunging several circles, go to the horse with your hobble and hobble him. Tighten your front cinch. You should use some judgement here. All we are doing is cinching him up tight enough so we can ride him. If you cinch him too tight, it will cause him to react more. But make sure that it's tight enough that you can get him rode. Take your hobbles off, and give him some more lunging. When he's settled down and going smoothly, he's ready to have his head tied around. Take your lunging line off and lead your horse to the center of the pen.

Take your left rein from the horn. Run this rein under your latigo wraps between your cinch ring and rigging ring. Then using your left hand pull your horse's head towards you to the left. At the same time taking up the slack in your rein with your right hand. Do this in easy stages a little at a time. Do not make this first tying of the colt's head to one side too short on the first trial. Bend his head just enough to where it's about a foot to one side out of line with that of his body. Then make a slip knot with your latigo rein to tie it off. The slip knot will make it easier later when you loosen his head from the tied position. Make sure that the loose rein on

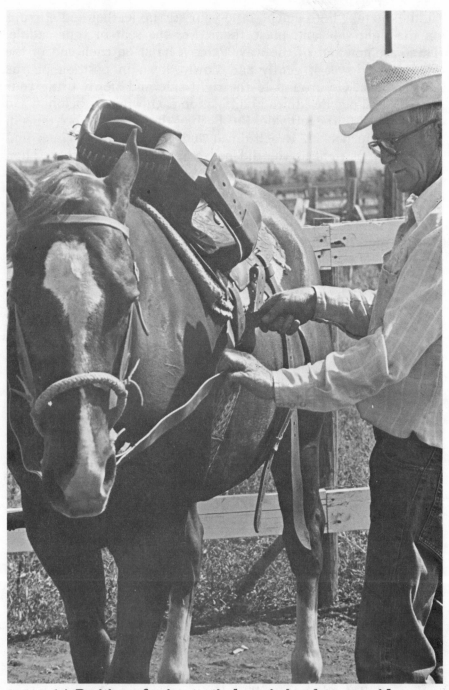

(a) Position of reins to tie horse's head to one side

Photography by Neil Mishler, Ponca, Nebraska

(b) First tie position;

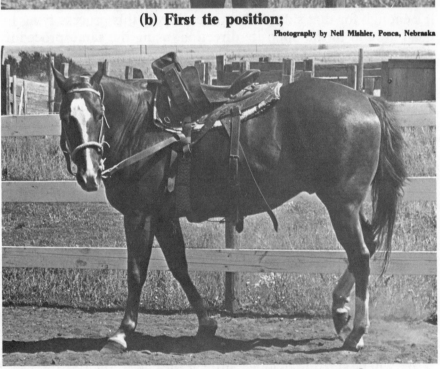

(c) Last tie position showing extreme angle

the right side of the horse gives him complete head freedom to the left, when the left rein is tied off. If the right rein that's attached to the horn does not permit complete head freedom to the left, remove it and lace it up under the right side of your hackamore head stall. Make sure it's secure enough that it won't loosen and fall down causing him to step on it.

If you tie the colt's head around at too sharp of an angle the first time, he could throw himself. It also might cost you a stirrup and a bruised side on the horse. Make this horse move around. Get behind his left shoulder as in lunging position. Make him move, all the while watching him closely.

When you see him giving with his head a little and not trying to go straight ahead and set solid in the hackamore, let him stop. Go up to him slowly. Loosen your rein and knot. Take up more slack, and bring the horse's head around towards you further. We want this horse in this next action to be going in a small circle. Get after him a little. Stay pretty close to his rear quarters and make him turn. Then let him set for a minute. He will stand with his head turned towards the tie. When you see a little slack in that tie rein, it's enough for that side at this time. Repeat this process tying his head around in the opposite direction, using the same procedure you used in tying his head to the left using two positions.

If the horse is exceptionally stubborn in this procedure, after shortening up his head the second time, and he still does not want to turn, take your lunging whip with you. When he gets to a corner of the pen or the fence go straight to the horse's head. Force him to turn away from you and the fence, then quickly get in front of him and make him turn again away from the fence. You can get a horse in a corner and every time he turns out of the corner take a step or two so you are behind his head, and you can make him keep turning in a tight circle. Don't whip him, just threaten him a little to induce him to turn. When he's bending pretty free both ways, he's ready for his first mounting.

We will not use spurs on this colt for the first two weeks even though we tape the rowels. What we will be trying for or shooting at is to get a walk, trot, on this colt. While we are doing this, we will also be getting some bends or turns on him. Not anything spectacular, but trying to start him being light and pliable in the hackamore with a rein in each hand.

We will be starting to lope a little at the end of the third week. If he's inclined to want to sooner, and doesn't do it out of fear or pressure, let him. Do not make him or let him do it too long. We will be more interested in getting him adjusted to carrying weight and teaching him to give lightly to the reins. You will not carry a bat these first days or the first week either unless he's a real lazy or doggie colt. We will use a lot of patience and little discipline to get him to do the things we want him to do. The main thing the first week is to get him in motion at a walk and trot around this pen. Turning him enough to start him turning both away from the fence to reverse the way he's headed, also turning him into the fence to accomplish the turns.

We have now finished tying his head around on both sides in our hackamore. Go to him, loosen your reins and lead him over to the center of the pen. Then put your hobbles back on him. Take your reins and run one end of your reins through the slot in the end of the other rein and tie it off. You can use a simple latigo over and under knot, or you can just plain knot them together. Place these reins around your saddle horn or even let them rest around the swells of your saddle. You also want them hanging loose, because you won't gather up your reins while setting on the horse for the first time. Check your hobbles on your horse. Make sure they won't come off. Now go around to the left side and face the same way the horse faces. If he is not roached and still has a mane, take your left hand and get a hold of a good chunk of the mane. Then standing in about where your back girth would be, place just the toe and half of the ball of your left foot in the left stirrup. Do not pick up your rein. Reach up with your right hand and grasp the right swell or horn of your saddle. If you are in close to your horse and have bent your knee high enough, you should be going almost straight up getting on. We will point out one thing here. We are not getting up on this horse to ride him. We are simply going to sit on him. Nor will you put your right boot in the right stirrup. What you will do is be prepared to leave or dismount from this horse if he jumps out. So as you go up, watch his eyes and ears and head. If he acts pretty steady, just set up there. Keep your left ball of your left foot in the left stirrup with your right foot free on the right side. You can step down if he jumps out real easy if you're ready. The main thing is to make sure you think to bail off and step down. Take pains you don't bump him with your stirrups. Relax up there. Start to pat and rub this horse, first on one side of his neck, then the other. Let's say after you have been up there two minutes, get down. Go around him a couple of times. Then get

Mounted position first time up on hobbled horse

Photography by Neil Mishler, Ponca, Nebraska

back up on him, doing the same things in the same way you did the first time. If he has not moved out or tried his hobbles while you're up there, you have gotten one of the more technical phases over with. He has now seen you up there. He has accepted it, or he would have tried to move out. You have got to be alert and stay ready. You can guess and be fairly accurate at what a horse might do, but you can never be positive.

72

Let's go back over this one more time. When you test this horse with these hobbles on, if he moves, get down and start over. If he moves the next time you attempt to mount him, just try standing straight up in your left stirrup while you pat or rub him. Don't get close to his poll or his ears. Confine your rubbing and petting to his neck. Go slow. Don't move in jerks.

Let us say you have now sat on him, and he hasn't made a move to jump out. Now get down slowly and untie the hobbles. Take and place this hobble around both front legs, but you will not take any twists in the center. I repeat "don't twist them in the center." Simply put them around the front legs. Then measure off your ends to even the hobbles, and tie one single knot in that sack hobble on the flat of the bone on his left front leg. Remember one single knot. Now from the time you dismounted from the horse with the hobbles secured, don't move the horse. Remember you now have him hobbled with just that one single knot. What we are doing here, and it will work, is making this horse think he's still hobbled securely. He doesn't know you have only the single knot on the hobble and no twists in the middle. We have fooled him,

(a) First step of horse coming out of hobble with single knot; (b) Coming out of hobble completed

Photography by Neil Mishler, Ponca, Nebraska

and he should stand quietly while mounting.

This time when you mount the horse, you will change your tactics. Leave your reins tied together, because you might drop one. If this happens on a colt, and you reach down to retrieve it, it could spook him. Measure off your reins making sure they are even. You also want your reins slack. Do not pull back on your reins when mounting the horse. Then get a handful of mane in the same hand as your reins using your left hand. Step up slowly and easily as you did the first two times in this process while the horse was hobbled. Once you're mounted, place both feet in your stirrups clear to your boot heels and just sit. Pat or pet this horse as you did before. Be careful of your reins when moving them up there from side to side. He is not used to them yet. That strap I recommended through the fork of your saddle may be useful at this point. Take a rein in each hand, and tie them together. Start to pull this horse's head to one side. If he doesn't come out of the hobble and move his legs, pull in the other direction gently to move him off center. He will come out of the hobble the first step he takes. When he takes the second one, he knows that he is not hobbled at this point. Pat and pet and rub the horse some more. Speak encouragingly to him in a soft voice. Then move him some more. All these first moves should be brief and either one way or the other, always to right or left—never straight ahead. When he acts like he will move out straight ahead at a walk on his own, let him do so.

(a) Hand position on first turns to right after coming out of hobble; (b) Hand position on left turn

Photography by Neil Mishler, Ponca, Nebraska

Now you will soon realize why we tied this colt's head around. Even one lesson at this will have convinced him to turn and give to the hackamore, because he could go no other way. So remember you have a rein in each hand and they are tied together. After you have mounted, and have placed both feet deep in the stirrups, adjust your reins doing it slowly, so that you do not spook him. Then holding the rein that you are going to make your horse turn with, say to the left, your hand position here should be a little lower than your thigh. This places the pull about where the pressure was applied while his head was tied around. If he doesn't come untracked or off center that way; pet him a little and try him the other way. Then keep repeating these procedures until he takes a step.

Now supposing it didn't go that way, and he decided that he might try to pitch. At the first sign of it, transfer your right rein to your left hand fast and get a hold of that strap. Don't pull too hard on those reins. Just a little. Set back to where your body is just back of center from being straight up. Don't clench your legs around the horse as he is not used to it. If you do this, it will further encourage him to hop. Just sit down. Lay that arm holding the strap across your right hip and pull back and not up on the strap. When the horse quits trying to buck, go back to a rein in each hand and keep bending him slowly a little at a time. Every time you get a turn on him, and he stops, pet him and speak softly. Say "Fine" or "good." Now you can start resting your legs a little tighter against the horse's body. We will not stay on this horse this first riding longer than ten or fifteen minutes.

Here's how to get off this colt. You will continue to dismount the following way for a week. If you got down in the same position as you did when mounting him, you would wind up just in front of his hind leg. If he jumped ahead and kicked, he could kick you. Here's how to avoid it. Loosen up your foot in your left stirrup. Put the ball and toe only in it. Take your left rein in your left hand about two and one-half feet from the hackamore. Take a firm grip on this rein. Don't pay any attention to your right rein. Now do this all in one motion. Put your right hand on the horn. Take your foot out of the right stirrup. As you come down, turn your body on the ball of left foot and aim at about a forty-five degree angle away from the horse's left shoulder facing your saddle until you're on the ground. Try to do this fairly smooth and slow. Step away from the colt at the same time. You might practice this on a gentle horse. If your colt does jump out, you have that left rein in your left hand, and as he hits the rein it will force his rear end away from you when he turns his head into you.

Everything we have done so far makes good sense. That's why it works. A rider has to learn to think ahead of his horse, and try to anticipate what the animal might do. Take every advantage you can, while at the same time not hurting the horse. They don't want to hurt you. What they do is with a defensive attitude rather than any intent to harm the rider.

From out of the old west comes this saying, "Don't pull leather. It's a disgrace." Forget it. Stay on your horse, pardner. We will show off after we get him broke. I've seen children where this thing of not hanging on, taught by people who were supposed to be riding instructors, instruct their pupils not to hang on; come what may. I've seen the same youngsters still clutching one side of their body with a free hand fall to the ground rather than take the precaution of trying to hang on. I would have told them to hang on when in a storm or do whatever they could do to protect themselves. Another common mistake riders make is when a horse rears up a little, they will pull harder on the reins to balance their body. Don't do it. If he comes up in front turn his head loose. You could pull him on up further, and he might come on over. What you do when the horse comes back to the ground with his front feet would be to rein him to one side or the other with a side pull using your hand pulling down and to the side. Then ride him off.

I would advise taking the grain ration away from your horse for the first ten days you ride him. Give him all the good quality hay he can eat. I've found the full grain ration on horses on these first saddlings will cause you to be working against a lot of spirit unnecessarily. Once you have the horse coming along well, you can start the grain again. At the beginning it will help your efforts to keep the grain from him.

 **9**

Further Lessons for Greenie

These next saddlings will be mostly a repetition of what we have done: Hobbling, putting on the hackamore, then the saddle, using blankets, and taking a lot of time doing it. Don't rush it. Be slow, smooth, deft, and direct in your movements. Stop occasionally to talk a little to the horse and pat him a little. Try to build a degree of confidence in him. Look at it from his point of view. Left to himself he would not be there at all. But he's a captive and everything you do with him is always new to him in the beginning. He is naturally suspicious of every new action. Give him time to adjust to it. Build up a relationship of just enough fear to make him try to do what you are trying to teach him, but also use only the minimum amount of discipline to get it done. Remember all we are trying to get done the first week on this horse is to: Set on him, get some turns on him, get him to walk out, get him used to our moving arms, the feel of our legs against his sides, and used to our weight which will take a month or more on the latter. We will not tie this horse's head around again on these sessions unless after having ridden him, he would refuse to turn one way or the other. I would then dismount and tie that side of his head around towards the direction he refused to turn. Rather than take a chance at this point on getting after him too hard or fighting him to make him do it while I was on him, I would tie his head around, until I was sure he was bending. Then untie your horse's head, but remember, rehobble him tight first with the twists in the hobble. Then move him over. Push him just a little to let him know he's hobbled. Then remove the hobble. Use the single knot without the twists and remount him. Repeat this method of getting on the horse for one week. For this one week, you will hobble him to saddle. Take them off to lunge. Then tie your single knot in the hobbles with no twists to get on and move out. After about ten sessions with hobbles, you will be tying this horse to the post, and be saddling him there without hobbles. You will be getting on without them also. It won't be long before you can lead him to your tie post, and saddle him up, and ride off without the hobbles.

As you advance the horse in his training, start to use your legs a little more, not forward of the cinch but straight down in the area of his belly. If the horse shows resistance to go forward bump him real easy with both legs. If that doesn't get reaction, put both reins in your left hand and with your free hand slap your thigh just enough to make a little noise and to get his attention. If he is not a real doggie colt, you should get results to urge him forward around the pen with legs and an occasional slap on your thigh. If he appears to be stubborn and is a real doggie colt, on your next saddling you will carry a bat. Again you won't stay on this horse at this session for more than thirty minutes. You can, however, do some ground work with him. Such as grooming, going around him and moving your stirrup leathers forward and backward.

One thing might be added here that we left out. Pay particular attention to this colt's feet. If he needs his hooves trimmed, and is too long, get the farrier to do this job if you do not know how to do it yourself. The horse's feet have to be in good shape to travel, especially with the added weight you are putting on him. You should also instruct this farrier at this time not to rasp this colt's feet down too much on the sole or bottom of his feet. I've been forced to lay horses up that were in training for as long as a week for this reason. I would not shoe the horse on his first six weeks of schooling, if I had good ground to work on. The reason being, that in his awkwardness during his first sessions of schooling, he could clip one of his legs with a shoe, causing a cut or bruise. If he's already shod and is used to shoes, go ahead with him. But make sure he has been reset and is not sore from a recent shoeing. Long toes on a horse, shod or unshod, can cause him to fall in his early schooling, because he does not have the same balance under weight that he would have otherwise.

The following saddlings should be more simple. You have determined how many blankets to use and about how tight to cinch him. In the cinching you should use a little caution, but you won't have to be so particular about it. You would do it twice. The first time, no tighter than to hold your saddle in place until you have lunged him. The second time to tighten more, prior to riding him. Reexamine that hackamore once more. Make sure your sheepskin is right, so you don't sore him up under the jaw. Also that the bosal of the hackamore is resting on the bridge of the nose of the horse.

If it's extremely hot, and as we have started to move the horse out a little faster, after we are through riding him, we will get a pail of lukewarm water, a big sponge, and also a metal sweat scraper. Use the scraper to wipe off excess water left by your sponge. If the horse has become real sweaty, and I mean any horse in hot weather, do not fail to wash him. We are not talking in terms of giving the horse a bath. We are intending on covering the area of the horse that has been exposed to the saddle and cinches, especially the front one. There's a lot of cinch rash occurring through the country. Use clean blankets, a good smooth cinch, and bathe those horses after riding. The colt is especially vulnerable to cinch rash because of his being tender on those spots where the saddle and cinch are. Run your hand over these places before you saddle up. If you feel some small pimples in the hair, you have already burnt him a little. If this horse that you are training is sensitive, he may blow up when you ride him on account of this cinch rash. You can see a bad case of it with the naked eye, but it will probably be seen only after he's been ridden with the rash affecting him and the chafed hide is starting to show some shedded hair. So take your hand and feel on each side where your front cinch contacts his skin, then over his entire back where the saddle would set. If you discover this rash, get a can of salve made for this condition and treat these spots wherever you find the pimples in the hair. If it's too bad and your horse reacts to being ridden, put him away. Lay him up until these scabs come off. You can't expect a colt to endure this pain and still accept his schooling without some undesirable results.

After about a week's riding, this horse should be walking out pretty freely around this breaking pen. We will even urge him into a slow trot for a few rounds in both directions. Then turn at a walk down through the middle of the pen coming out the other direction. Cut down the center at about the same spot coming and going out in the opposite direction. Do not stop this horse or try to at this time by pulling on both reins. If he stops, and you have not tried to stop him, urge him forward. Because at this point we are trying to get across to him to move forward. If you do stop him, do so by pulling on one rein, the one that is next to the fence. Say "whoa," then pull his nose towards the fence. He will stop. Now you've asked him to stop, and you can reward him at this point with a pause, perhaps thirty seconds. Then pat him and go on. After a week's lessons do not pat or pet him when he stops on his own. Anything contrary to what we are trying to teach this horse from now on, we will not reward by voice or touch. Nor will we discipline too much either for not doing it. He won't accept, nor should he have to, very much discipline this first week. Our main objectives during this time are: (1) Saddling him. (2) Lunging him. (3) Getting him to move out at a walk. (4) Perhaps a little trotting. (5) Some turns. Be satisfied with a little progress each day. Remember short sessions, a little progress and put him away.

While you have been riding this colt, you should have been watching your hand positions. Your pull on your hackamore reins is back towards and below your thighs. You will also start to hold your hand away from your body, but still in line with the pull on his nose. Make sure when you pull on one rein, your other rein is completely loose. This will give your horse the opportunity of having complete head freedom. You will be teaching him to watch the hand that's making the pull, and at the same time, the pull will cause the bosal action to be on his nose and not under his jaw. In other words, we have already started to get this horse to turn without raising his head.

Let us say that the doggie colt is the kind of horse you're working. Despite efforts with bumping him a little with your legs or even a lot, he does not seem to want to move out like he should, and the thigh slapping didn't work either. We carried a bat along for this purpose on this session. Attempt to make the colt move out again. If you fail, do the following: Put your right rein in your left hand with the other one. Take out the slack in your reins but don't pull. Tap the colt lightly with the bat. If he moves out in any direction, don't use it again, until he stops again. Before you use it again, try your legs, and also slap the popper of the bat on your leg. The noise might help influence him. If that doesn't work this time you will pop him harder on the rump. As soon as your horse responds, get that right rein back in your right hand. Make these moves with these rein hands fast and smooth. If he's starting to go along fairly well, I'd put my bat back on the saddle horn and on a skittish colt I'd put the part hanging down under my leg.

If the colt is reluctant to turn at all or isn't really trying, take a shorter rein in the direction you're going to turn. Put your other rein with some slack in it in the same hand you're trying to turn with. Then take your bat and touch him with it on the rump on the outside of the turn. He cannot see the bat hand when it touches him, because his head is turned in the opposite direction. This will have the effect of him watching your rein hand, and make him realize that you have some discipline following behind the pull. Later on we will use it on his neck just in front of his shoulder, but not at this time.

As these procedures have been followed, we have made progress by the end of the first week. We have walked and trotted him. He is turning with a less heavy pull on the hackamore rein. In the second week we will bring into play some figure eights the size of the pen, in an area where our eights will be confined to about forty feet by thirty feet. After you have lunged him and ridden around the pen three or four times in each direction, we will start to make these figure eights using a big area. In order to do this right, you have got to look up ahead of you and pinpoint in your mind each time where you're going to turn. Try to go in such a manner where your figure eights are equally divided. Down the middle should be easy. Aim at the same spot each time when you are making these eights at a walk. Do the same thing at a trot.

It's about time, I think, to talk a little about the neck stop. In these schooling sessions you will be doing a lot of stopping for short periods. If we teach this horse a neck stop, which we can do in two weeks' time, it will enable us to make these many stops possible without hauling our horse's nose, jaw, or mouth. It is a cue, and anybody can teach it. To accomplish this, when you are riding the horse around at a walk in the pen (we are talking about the full area in use), do these things in this order. When you want to stop your horse, pick out a point you are going to stop. Shorten up on the rein next to the fence prior to getting to that spot, but don't pull until you get there. Say "whoa" to him clear and sharp. Follow up by pulling on that rein next to the fence. As you finish with the pull, take your left hand with the rein still in it (or the one away from the wall or fence) and place your hand on the horse's neck, just in front of your saddle. If you have a jumpy horse, do some ground work on his neck in that area. If you don't, and he's spooky, it might cause him to jump out when you put your hand there. When the stop is completed, pet the horse. Reward him with your voice saying, "Fine, good." Let him set about a minute and start over. Now let's go over one more time how this is going to go. Look ahead. Pick a spot where you're going to stop. Say "whoa."

Pull your horse's head towards the fence. At the same time you will take the off rein hand and touch this horse on the top of his neck. Don't leave it there. Remove your hand as soon as the horse stops. Relax and pause for a minute. You will do this going both directions at a walk for about five times in each direction. That's enough for that day. You will find the next day, the horse will be stopping at the word "whoa." Don't repeat this word over and over. Say it once and follow through with the other two measures. Then when you're getting response at a walk, try them at a trot. You will find that the first measure that you can eliminate will be the side pull into the wall to stop. It won't be long before you can eliminate the "whoa," and he will stop with the hand touch on his neck. Then at the first response on this neck touch, you will employ it just before you say "whoa." You will get results. We are not trying to get this horse to set down. We are merely trying to get him to stop without pulling or saying "whoa" or both. Later on it will be valuable when we are teaching a horse leads and leg pressure. When your horse has learned to stop on this neck touch, he will have done it for the following reasons: His first signal to stop was the rein forcing his head towards the wall. He then heard the command "whoa." Then by placing your thumb down over his neck and your other four fingers being felt on the other side (like a slingshot crotch). He puts them all together and finally settles for the neck touch as he wanted to stop for a minute anyway.

In writing about this neck stop, I'm not trying to tell you, you won't be using a pull on the reins later to stop this horse. What I'm trying to get across to you is this fact. In this day and age of horse training where you are riding your horse daily in training for performance, you will be stopping many times and starting over, correcting mistakes, switching from one maneuver to another. The neck stop will eliminate many hundreds of hard pulls on the mouth of your horse after he is bitted. If taught in the hackamore, he will for sure respond to the same method in the bit.

Figure Eights, Beginning of Neckreining, and Backing Up

As we finish the second week of riding the colt, let us look back over the way he has responded to what we were trying to teach him, and at what points, if any, he is not making progress in his training. Let us say it is a simple thing now to hobble the horse. He has accepted them. He is standing quiet when we have saddled him. He will not move away from us when we exchange the halter for the hackamore. If this can be done, we are getting a lot accomplished. If he has tried to jump away from us while doing any of the above things, we would then take him over the the snub post, tie him and then hobble him prior to saddling him. This would be a disciplinary measure to convince him he must stand. We will still not pull the cinch up at this time, any tighter than to keep the saddle on him while we lunge him. I would, however, untie him to put the hackamore on him. I would rather have his head free when I put the hackamore on him or bridle. If he is tied to the post whether hobbled or not, he will in most instances move back in the halter. This will make the tie rope come just about in the position where your left hand is trying to open his mouth and slip the bit in his mouth. So untie him when putting your riding head gear on him, whether it be a snaffle bit or hackamore, but while he is still in the hobble.

Now let us say when lunging him he's going good in one direction, starting out at a walk, and breaking into a trot, and finally into a lope without any trouble. If the horse, during this period, is still making an attempt to pitch a little each time prior to riding him, we will keep lunging him until he has stopped it, and is moving freely in the circle. Were you to try to ride this type of colt without the lunging, he would very likely try to pitch to some degree when first mounting him. You lead him around a few minutes before mounting, especially if you ride him without the lunging. If he is not trying to hump while lunging and moves out freely without humping at all, I'd figure this horse was a pretty solid, honest kind of a horse and would treat him accordingly. On the other hand if he continued to want to pitch in the first steps or starts on the line, I would take the slack out of both reins and half hitch them to the horn of the saddle. Don't have them tight, but just loose enough that every time he lowers his head to hop, his nose will hit the hackamore. It won't be long before it will discourage him from doing it. You also use your lunge line in this operation. Simply attach it to the lower part of the hackamore and proceed to lunge him with the reins tied to the horn. Most colts aren't this way, but occasionally you will run into one that is. While he is attempting to pitch on the line with the reins tied up, I would get after him with my lunging whip and force him into it a littler harder, because the quicker he learns there is nothing to be gained in this direction, the quicker he will quit. Rough him up a little on that session. Then the next time start him off as easy as you can, so he knows he has an option. If he doesn't try to hop, he won't get hurt. But when he does try it and wants to use force to resist us, he's met with force. He will soon straighten out.

It's always seemed a little strange to me but these lessons on the ground hardly, if ever, are blamed on the trainer by the horse. I think he blames it on the equipment and does not associate it with the trainer. If the horse after the second week is trotting and turning in slow turns, and has been loped out a little on the line and it isn't bugging him, I'd say we were making good progress in our second week with him. Hopefully we will have rewarded him when he's doing good by voice and petting him. We have given him minimum discipline with voice and restraint on our reins when he's doing wrong. We have now started a good relationship with the pupil. As we get our minds focused in the same direction, things should progress from here on out at a fairly rapid pace.

In the first week we had limbered the horse's neck up. He should be giving his head freely and easily each way with either rein. We should be able to turn him around in a tight little circle to left or right. We want this horse to walk when we want to walk, and only trot when we ask him to. This should be started on the second week. We start at a walk and if at any time, he starts to trot when we want to walk, pull him down to a walk right away. Don't wait and let him get the idea that he has a choice on his own or do a combination of both whenever he chooses to do so. After he's walked and is not breaking into a trot, we will then give him a cue to trot. Lean a little forward. Give him some slack in both reins and induce him to trot by pushing both legs against his sides straight down from your hips. Bump him with your legs, not hard but lightly. Once he is trotting, let him choose his own speed. In most cases he will ease into it, and will not have to be pulled down. However, if it does happen that he is trotting too extended, pull him down to the desired speed. Gradually get off your reins and let him proceed. Five or six times around the pen is enough. Now walk a few rounds, then cue for a trot again going in the opposite direction.

We will continue to figure eight this horse. Again I will stress that you make these eights right. We are striving to get some precision on his pattern of travel. You can also crowd in a lot more turns in reining training using the little eights which will tend to make the horse more flexible, and cause him to learn to gather a little on the turns. In order to do this, you will have to look up and ahead of you. In other words, you will be choosing the exact course at all times for the horse to follow. Don't let him choose it. You do it. You will also be teaching this horse control while it's going on.

Choose your first circle to be what you would consider big enough to be made easily. Start at a walk. Walk that circle five or six times in the same size or as near as you can guess. Of course, it would be on one side of the pen or the other leaving enough room for a circle of the same size on the other side. After having gone in the one half of the figure eight several times, stop in the center. Pause a few seconds. Then proceed in the other circle in the opposite direction. When you have done this at a walk several times going in each direction on the circles, you should have been trying to make both circles even. In other words, don't make one circle small and the other larger. Try to make them both as even as possible.

We will now do them at a jog or slow trot. When you come down the center of the figure eight do what is known as a flat eight. Make sure your horse has come a length and one-half of his body in a straight line down through the middle of the eight. Trot two or three times one way in one circle, then break him off and make three or four circles in the other direction. Stop in the center of the eight every time you stop. Use your neck stop to stop the horse. You can now use both hands to touch his neck in front of the saddle. If he does not stop, pull your hands straight back one

Horse starting to neckrein using proper hand position

Photography by Neil Mishler, Ponca, Nebraska

across each thigh. Let him rest awhile after each eight or nine figure eights.

The horse at this time will start to break off on his own at the center of the figure eight. It looks good but is not right. When he is tempted to do this, go back to trotting the single circle and do not let him break off to turn on and start the other until cued or reined to do so. You will employ these figure eights from here on out in every training session for about fifteen minutes.

Now you have gotten the figure eights pretty well in your head and probably the horse's. You should start paying a lot of attention to what you have been doing with your hands, while this has been going on. When changing directions with the horse, you should have been doing the following: As you held out the hand for the horse to see, prior to the side pull, and away from your body you should have laid the other rein, which would be the neckrein, lightly against the other side of his neck. You will leave it there very lightly and not be pulling back on it, while his attention is directed on your hand that is pulling him into the circle. If he fails to turn into the hand shown him after applying the neckrein, use that hand to snap the hackamore just a little on his nose. Then pull him lightly into the circle line. He will soon realize that to avoid the little sharp tug on the hackamore, he has to turn. When he does it, don't snap or tug. The next time around give him a chance to do it on his own. If he doesn't do it, repeat the snap until he does. Every time he does two or three either way by answering the neckrein, stop in the center of the eight and reward him. By the end of the week, he should be starting to get the neckrein figured out. But do not go to two reins in one hand. Forget about it, as we will continue to use the rein in each hand for a long time to come. The only time we will go to the two reins in one hand is to run a test on the horse to see how he is progressing on his neck reining or for protection in case of a storm. You may have to use that strap we mentioned that's through the fork of your saddle. Now you are becoming aware of the formula to teach the horse to neckrein with a rein in each hand. Don't get snap simple with your hackamore reins. Use only enough to assure you that the horse is making progress. Don't try to do it all today. Don't be a weekend trainer or try to accomplish on one weekend what it would take a trainer to do in two weeks. You will be pushing your horse too fast and expecting too much.

Do these things like you have all the time in the world. That's the impression you should give the horse. Remember, if you do this job right, when you wind up, you will have a good head position on your horse from these methods. Your second horse will be a lot easier, and by the time you have ridden about three hundred or better different horses, you will be able to write a book yourself.

One thing to bear in mind, that the use of that inside hand is what positions your horse's head. The sharp tug on the hackamore is the only discipline you have with hands and reins. Never pull back hard on both of them at the same time. It's either one rein or the other except when we are teaching the horse to back up.

I will point out at this time that these figure eights are important. If done correctly they will accomplish the following: They will teach the horse a precise line of travel. They will teach the horse control, and will teach him to obey the rein signals. In the first stages of his riding, we did not apply the neckrein, but in our figure eights, once the horse was doing them well on a side pull with a rein in each hand, we started the neckrein procedure. When we first apply the neckrein, we did not expect any response to it. Little by little by applying the neckrein first as a signal to turn in the opposite direction, then following it up with a sharp pull on the opposite rein, we will start to get some response to the neck-rein. After the horse is starting to respond, over a period of time, we improve the response by the disciplinary snap and pull of the direct rein opposite the neckrein. This is a gradual transfer from the direct to the indirect rein which is the neckrein. While using the rein in each hand method along with the hackamore, it enables us to keep the proper head position on the horse while the training is going on. We have also gone through this procedure without injuring the horse's mouth.

From here on out we will apply the neck rein first. If we don't get results, we give that hackamore a light snap with the opposite rein. Remember, do not push on the neck rein hard. Use just enough pressure where we know he can feel it. Nor will we pull back on the neck rein while applying it. If we pull hard on this neck rein at the same time pushing it against his neck, we are applying pressure on the bosal in the wrong place which would be under his jaw. You are giving the horse an excuse to raise his head. We want to avoid this. It might be a good place to put in a few words here, snaffle bit versus hackamore. You would not be able to jerk this snaffle, but would have to take a steady and sometimes hard pull to get the same thing accomplished. All the while you are tugging on the colt's mouth. You are not going to make his mouth any better by doing it. You have lost a means of discipline in the snaffle bit that you could only achieve with the hackamore without applying pressure on his mouth. You would, however, use your snaffle bit and reins about the same way as you would with your hackamore reins, which we will do later when we bit the horse up coming out of the hackamore. But we will be stopping the horse with the neck stop and an easy pull on the reins. He will be backing up and neckreining. We have gotten all this done in a two-month period and have not had to make one pull on his mouth to accomplish it, as we have been using only the hackamore.

Study these past few pages about the neck reining several times. Try to instill it in your memory, so that when you go to apply it on the horse you will not be making a lot of false moves with your hands and reins that will confuse the horse. Remember, you have to think ahead of your horse, and what actions you are going to

Backing up, first stages showing position of hands

Photography by Neil Mishler, Ponca, Nebraska

apply with your hands, arms, and legs. Do them the same every time and concentrate on what you are doing and on the horse. Don't have a lot of rail birds on the fence asking you questions or giving you advice. There are many people who let their conversation travel away ahead of their knowledge in trying to influence you and build up their ego on strictly imaginary advice. Avoid them. They mean well, but you are far better off to take an experienced trainer's advice.

At the end of the second week of the horse's training, when you are about to quit your training session, which has been probably in the area of an hour by now, sit on the horse and relax. After having sat on him a couple of minutes, have petted him a little, and he's standing quiet, take a rein in each hand on your hackamore. Holding your hands about even with your thighs pull straight back on his nose. Say "back" to him, clear and sharp. Hold him in the hackamore without giving slack to his head. Use the amount of pressure needed. Some horses will stand for about a minute. Then they will back one faltering step to relieve the pressure on their nose. Now this is important, on the first step back, even if it is only one foot in distance, release your pressure right away. Pat him, and give him a "good boy" or "fine." Make a big thing of it. Let him set for a minute. Then repeat. If he fails to give, pull straight back on both reins. Then pull harder on one rein. This will cause him to come off center one-half step. Then release your reins. Set a spell and repeat it in the other direction. If he moves off center, release your pressure. Reward him and pause or dwell. Then try it straight back again. If you get one or two steps the first lesson, quit and take it up on the next session. I find I have better success when a horse has been ridden awhile than when he's fresh to start to teach him to back up. If these aforementioned methods don't work, try this one. While on the ground stand about even with your stirrup on the left side of your horse. Run your right rein to your right hand, the rein resting in your hand on the seat of your saddle. Your left hand will hold the left rein. Now tighten up your reins, holding your left rein above your waist. Pull back using the command "back." You can apply a lot of pressure on his nose in the hackamore in this position. It will get most horses to start backing up. Remember the first step he takes back, release your pressure on his nose and on your reins. Reward him. Again, a couple of steps a day and add to them. At every step he takes back, release your reins and take up for another step.

One other method that will work on a real stubborn animal is to take about enough baling wire to make three or four wraps around the exact center of the top of the bosal. Make sure where you twist it with the pliers to tighten and hold it that the twist is at the top so it does not touch his nose. Remove this wire from the bosal when this part of his training is finished. While using it, don't overuse it. When you first apply the pressure to the horse, start the pull on the reins lightly giving the horse a chance to respond. Then increase the pressure if he does not. This will work on the ground or when you are mounted. I would rather use it than the bat across his chest, because any excess use of the whip or bat on the ground tends to make a horse suspicious of the handler or trainer. Common sense has to be used at all times, and take your time.

When we progress in our backing of the horse in its final stages, which will be quite a ways down the road from what we have covered, one of our major objectives will be getting it done right. We will be keeping the following things in mind. We will want the horse to back straight. The horse in his first efforts to back is very awkward. He will use one back leg to get it done. As he comes back, he will favor one leg or the other to take a full step and will use the other to follow it. He will also make a shorter step back with one leg or the other. This causes him to go back in a circle instead of straight back as he would be doing if he used both hind legs evenly to back. When he backs straight, he will be using both hind legs evenly. When we have come along far enough where he is taking seven or eight steps back, by looking back in the direction of his rear quarters, we can determine which leg he's using to take the shortest step. We will turn the horse's front quarters in the opposite direction while still asking the horse to keep backing. This can only be done right with a rein in each hand. As he comes back, catch the direction of the curve he's making as soon as possible. Then pull his head over forcing him to use the other leg. It won't be long before he will use both legs evenly and will back straight.

We will also want this horse to back on a light rein with his nose down and mouth closed. Here again the hackamore works well as he does not have any reason to open his mouth, as he would in the snaffle. By keeping our hand positions low with a rein in each hand, we can teach him to tuck his nose as he backs up. He will also have a cue to know when he's expected to back. If he does not have a cue prior to pulling on the reins, he will, in most cases, be surprised and will raise his head when first pulled into backing, and in most cases not lower his nose at all in the process. Many a pleasure horse, after having done real well in everything else, has left a bad impression on a judge at the lineup when asked to back up. We will get into the reversing cues when we go to spurs on the green horse later on. The truth is you can keep a horse backing straight by the use of spurs. You can also drive him back with them, after he takes his first step back, just as you move him out by their use going ahead. He can also be cued with them when used right in signaling him to back. This will take the pressure off the reins to get him to do it.

 **11**

Loping and Further Reining

If you have your horse coming along to the point where you are: (1) Saddling, cinching up, and can take your halter off and put it around his neck while putting your head gear on. (2) You can lead him around for five minutes without lunging him. (3) He then walks off without any problem when you mount him. (4) If he is walking around inside of the pen without trying to trot only when you cue him. (5) He is hitting the little figure eights pretty well at a trot; he's ready to do some light loping from a trot for short intervals. We will start to urge this horse into a gallop. He has been lunged enough where he has the way he is going pretty well fixed in his mind in the breaking pen. It is at this time you should use a little caution. The movement of your body at a lope or gallop will sometimes cause the horse to react differently than he would at a walk or trot. So it's at this point, and the difference the horse feels from your body movement that he might react by trying to pitch a little or even hard. He might even run from this first experience at loping him. So start out going the direction in his natural lead that you have lunged him in. Put both reins in one hand, then cue him for a trot and gradually push him into a lope. On this first try and when the horse has made several circles around the pen at a lope, stop him and pet him. Reward him in this first attempt. Walk him around the pen. Then break into a trot and again urge him into a lope. About five or six successful endeavors at this time is enough for that session. If he is going faster than a slow lope, I would not try pulling him down to slow his gait unless I felt he was trying to run off. At this time all we are trying to get done is to get him to gallop and encourage him to do so. Then when he gets accustomed to the feeling caused by our weight and his different gait, we can start to slow him down. However, once the horse does start to lope, you can go back to a rein in each hand, as the taking of the reins in one hand was a protective measure in case you needed to get to that strap to stay on him. The first attempt to gallop might spook him and might cause him to duck off or reverse his position quickly. Most of the time it doesn't happen that way. He might show some surprise at the new gait with you on him, but as you have been riding him for some time, he will probably get right into it without too much trouble.

Let's now go back aways and think about the fact that we have only lunged this horse to the left, which is probably his natural lead at a lope. He readily lopes with the empty saddle on at the end of a lunge line. But we have not worked the horse in the other or off lead at a lope. We have also been able to urge this horse into a lope while riding him into his left lead. He is maintaining it for two or three circles. Once you have him hitting pretty good from a trot into the lope, it's now time to start thinking about the other lead, which of course, is going to be the hardest for you to teach him.

Even though you can now get on this horse and go with him, without all the preliminaries such as hobbles, lunging, etc., it would be wise unless you have had a lot of experience in the area of putting leads on horses, to put this horse back on the line and work with him each day before riding him on his off lead. At least long enough to where he is picking the correct lead up from a trot into a lope. Then while riding him, work both leads until he's doing them both well from a trot into a lope. To accomplish this, however, means that you will be working this horse over an extended period of time to get this job done. This means a lot of different sessions.

After we have accomplished getting this horse to take a right or left lead from trot to gallop in a circle in the starting corral, it is now time to think about getting him to take a right or left lead into a lope from a walk. This can be done best, in my opinion, by taking the horse along a wall or fence and going in a straight line on your first attempts. This would call for a longer distance to work in than you would have in your breaking pen. It can also be accomplished in the pen, if you have had enough experience at it.

We are now ready to change our tactics somewhat. We are going to concentrate on getting the horse to start on a left or right lead at a lope. Before we attempt to do this the horse should be going into a right or left lead from a trot to a lope in a circle. Our first step will be to get the horse to lope out on either lead from a walk into a gallop using a straight line. The horse will be walking, but we will

94

not cue for a trot, then break into a gallop. It's a gallop at this stage that we will want to start in. At first he will start faster than he will later. At this point what you are trying to teach the horse is to go into the gallop from a walk. Pay no attention to his leads. Either one doesn't matter, because we are going in a straight line. Get this done by leaning ahead a little, putting weight on your stirrups to get your weight off his loins. Touch him lightly with the spurs. Then once he starts, get a hold of him just a little with your reins, not enough to make him slow to a trot, just enough to ride smoothly and slow down enough where he is not running. Don't ride him at a gallop too far. Fifty or sixty feet is enough. Then use your neck stop and your reins to stop. Remember, touch a hand on his neck. Wait a second. Then come back on both reins low about waist high. Walk awhile, then repeat.

The reason you walk before each attempt to gallop is made is to keep the horse from thinking he's going to run fast. To impress on his mind that he's going into that lope from a walk rather than from a trot. About six or seven of these moveouts from a walk to lope or gallop, and after having worked it in with other things you have taught him should cover about a week's work. He should be moving out pretty freely when given his head at the start and squeezed with your legs and a light touch with the taped rowels on your spurs.

This is about the time to acquaint the horse to the spurs. If you have never used or worn spurs, but have done what we mentioned in our previous writing, you should have some knowledge about them. But here are some follow-ups about them: If you are inexperienced, you must tape your rowels. You should practice from the beginning in your riding to hold your spurs away from your horse at all times. You should not do this by pushing your feet out and ahead in your stirrups, but rather with your feet down behind the front cinch and in line with your hips so that you have a little bend in your knees, enough where when you push down on your stirrups that you can raise up out of your saddle one and one-half to two inches maximum. This is a good riding position for balance and leg grip.

People who have learned to ride bareback and have done so for a long time, have a tendency to use their legs and heels to cling to the horse, moreso, if the horse makes a wrong move that requires a quick reaction on the rider's part to stay on the horse's back. I will not contest the many times written article on "Heels Down

Position in Riding Technique." As to my own experience I have found any time I lower my heels (with or without spurs on) by bringing the heels of my boots down and my toes up, I find myself pushing ahead on my stirrups. This is in direct contrast to riding my balance. What we are talking about here is, if we keep our feet a little more straight in the stirrups, we will be pushing straight down on our stirrups to support our weight. At the same time we will be able to keep our spurs away from our horse's sides. You will have to practice this. But I'm sure once you acquire it, you will not go back to the other way of riding. By learning to ride this way you will also find that you will not be squeezing the sides of your horse as much. You will be leaving his sides more acceptable to leg cues when you will be using them later.

Another thing that happens to people not used to wearing spurs is if the horse makes a sudden or unexpected move, the rider reacts by immediately clenching his legs into the horse and around his middle, and with his toes out, grips with both legs and heels around the horse's belly. Well, you can almost imagine what's going to happen at this point. Both spurs are slammed into the horse's belly, and if he is not a dead head, he will react. What you should do if you are schooling the horse is to try to avoid doing what we described above. After having transferred your reins to one hand grasp the fork of your saddle. Keep your spurs out of your horse. Grip with the calves of your legs, holding your feet straight below them. Then when you have the horse back under control, go back to your original position with a rein in each hand. Your main worry if spurs are new to you will be when leaning on your horse when he's going in a fairly small circle, you will bring your inside spur against him on the inside of the turn and you don't know you are doing it. It also means you're overbalancing your weight to the inside. You are out of position. Study what I've written here. It's all tried and true. It will happen to you sooner or later. So think about it. Ride your horse and keep your weight in the middle of him. Don't throw it around.

I will also mention about the ball of the foot being used for balance. I'll not say that it has no place in riding the English horse, nor will I say it's not a preventative to the boot going into and through the stirrup. But in training your horse Western, you will want to keep your boot in the stirrup. I would seriously question whether you could keep them there by riding the stirrup with the ball of the foot very long on some of the movements required of the performance horse other than the well broke and trained pleasure horse. You need all the stirrup you can get. Even then you can occasionally lose one. I do recommend the wide deep roper-type stirrup for training other than the cutting horse. I also suggest you put your boot in clear to the heel. You will find that it gives you more support in your balance to get off your horse's loins to help him. That right stirrup with its weight will be there when you put your right foot down into it. It will also enable you to mount the green one easier with less risk of sticking your toe in him. It will give you more support while mounting him. I've used and tried all kinds. The narrow bottomed ox-bow stirrup for cutters and bronc riders, and possibly barrel racers is in their favor. But for training, the one I described suited my purposes the best. If I wanted to pop the horse on the shoulder to induce him to move over a little quicker, the weight and flat surface of the stirrup sure helped.

If the horse at the end of a month is starting to get the neck-reining ideas across, you can also start a little program of reining against the wall or fence, using the fence as a means of getting him to gather up his hind legs under him to make a turn against the fence. Every time he is turned into the fence to reverse his position to go in the other direction, the fence will make the horse take a step or two backwards. In our earlier stages of this colt's training, we have deliberately stayed a couple of feet away from the fence so that he had ample room to make these turns unhindered. But as we increased his knowledge of neckreining and lightness in the hackamore, we have now arrived at the stage where we are trying to get the horse to gather up more on his hindquarters when we make the turns. The training area fence can be used to a big advantage here. The fence will cause him to put his weight more on his hindquarters and with a little practice enable him to come around lightly with his front quarters. He can also learn to do a half or full pivot using the fence. It will make the horse lighter in his entire movements. I would suggest bringing this into play in each session from here out for not more than five minutes. If you have a square pen you are working in, it has an advantage over the round one, but the round one can be used in this procedure.

In the early stages of the horse's neck reining training, we have started on flat eights and small circles and extending it to just turns. We put our hand out for the horse to see as a signal to turn in that direction. The neck rein was then applied lightly across his neck on the opposite side. If he didn't respond to the neckrein, we gave a little snap and tug to the direct rein as a means to get him to respond to the neckrein. We stayed with this process until every time the neckrein was applied on one side of the horse's neck, we immediately saw the nose and muzzle of the horse turn in the opposite direction of the neckrein, then followed by his body into the turn. For this fence turning procedure, we will change our tactics at the beginning. We cannot expect this horse to neckrein and make a turn close to a wall or fence by using the same neck-reining technique as we used for the slow turns out in the open area. These turns close to the fence that we are trying to accomplish are much sharper and will call for much more effort on the horse's part.

With a hackamore rein in each hand, start down the fence. As you come into the corner, pull on the rein next to the fence. As the horse comes to a stop, as he will have to do before or in the process of turning, hold that pull rein solid. Then lay your neck rein lightly against his neck. As he reaches the point where he's gathered up behind trying to make the turn, bump him with your outside leg to push him into the turn. Your right leg next to the fence should be held in a squeezing position against the side he is turning into. Do this at a walk a few times, then at a trot, first one way then the other. Bring this fence turning maneuver into your training session for a short time every day. But don't lope him doing it until you have done it for about two weeks, walking and trotting. It won't be long before he will be coming off the ground in front to make the turn. Once he is that far don't overdo it, as he is putting a lot of weight on his hindquarters to get it done. You will also be improving his reining training at the same time. If he's not a broncy-type horse, you might raise your opposite boot away from the turn, and bump him on the shoulder with your stirrup. It won't hurt him, but will influence him to turn. It doesn't take a horse long when he feels your inside leg start to hug him in the belly and the pull on the rein that you are to wind him around the leg next to the fence. This is his first cue that you're going to turn. Then the inside rein being pulled, followed by the neckrein. Do not attempt this fence work until you think the horse is ready for it. He should be neckreining and loping out fairly well before starting it.

Once you are picking up the true lead and loping pretty freely you can take this horse out into a bigger arena. Do not go out and start into a lope. Just walk him and let him look at everything in the arena alone, with no other riders present, and no loose horses along any of the fences that make up the arena. Then after having just walked around, start to do the things you did in the breaking pen. You can walk some figure eights, trot some figure eights, but do not gallop your horse the first two or three times out. If you are in an inside arena, you probably could, but I would wait three or four sessions. I would also give this horse a pretty good lunging before venturing out, as well as riding him awhile in the breaking pen. If somebody there has a good quiet, well-mannered horse, follow him out. Ride around with him a few times. Your horse will follow the other horse and will have an opportunity to explore the area to get used to it.

Remember one other thing, by getting all those turns bending the horse around our leg, we have taught the horse that he has to turn with the side pull while in the hackamore. This is the means you would use to get your horse stopped when out in the bigger area you are riding him in. Your chances of getting him stopped if he is spooked are far better by pulling him around in a tight little circle until he stops than by pulling straight back on both hackamore reins. This would apply to a snaffle bit and reins as well as the hackamore. The reason we have stayed in the breaking pen for this length of time is so we have this horse pretty well controlled and that we don't have to take so many chances to get fouled up when we get into a bigger area. It is easier to get a horse to submit to control three to one times better in a small area as compared to a large one.

The Cow or Ranch Horse

In the process of writing this book, I've failed to mention where I would end the show training of this horse in order to make a good ranch horse out of him instead. I'm going to devote a few pages in that direction. I broke and trained ranch horses before I ever started to train show horses.

You can follow all the instructions in this book up to the time we started putting leads from walk to gallop, calling for a right or left lead. At this point I would cut out that portion of the training, including the reining training for the competition horse. I would concentrate on getting a sharp neck rein on the horse using the described methods. I would also work on a good reverse on the ranch horse. This is sure going to be a big advantage to be able to help the horse when first introduced to cattle.

I would also work this horse on cattle in a big pen, using a rein in each hand to get him to watch cattle. I would keep working on him to the point where when a cow is brought out of the herd, the horse would be starting on his own to keep this cow's head pointing away from him.

When this point is reached with the horse, the cutting horse trainer stops this procedure and wants a turn back man to turn the critter back so it's facing the cutter. From here on the trainer wants the cow to be face to face with his horse. This also is where the cutting horse will score the most points, but for a ranch horse, he does not have to stay off the cow and prepare to block head to head in most cases. I also believe to bring the horse to the stage where he is looking at a cow or yearling and keeping the critter going away from him on his own will have a good effect in his becoming a good ranch rope horse later on. He will stay with and behind a critter when she's bending better than a horse not worked on cattle prior to roping. I would also teach the neck stop to the horse. These things will save you a lot of aggravation when you go out to round up stock on greenie the first few times in the open.

 **12**

Collection, Leads, and Cues

If your breaking pen is large enough to lope a horse freely in, and when you have lunged him successfully at a lope going both directions, as well as riding him at a lope from a trot, it then should be okay to start him on his leads from a walk into the lope. This part of his schooling, however, is going to be much more difficult for him, and a lot more difficult for him to accomplish. On our previous efforts to teach him to lope, he has been extended and is what I call "jumping into the lead." We are now going to start him into a collected way of going into the lead, and also our choice of right or left lead from a walk.

From here on out we will start to discourage the horse from trotting prior to his beginning of the lope. Let's say this is the first real effort on our part to attempt to get this horse to go from a walk into a lope. We will first give our equipment a full examination before we start. Is our saddle right on the horse's back? Is our hackamore right on his nose? Is there a two-inch slack at the bottom of it? Is our sheepskin in place? Is the bottom of his jaw or chin sore? Can we put a couple of fingers between his withers and the gullet of the saddle? Have stirrup adjusting buckles been giving us any trouble scraping the sides of the horse? Are our reins right? Has the horse been making progress in his neck reining? Has he been doing the little figure eights smoothly? Can we back him up six or seven steps? Have we gotten the horse into a gallop fifteen or twenty times? If so, we are ready to proceed on the leads.

Mount up. Ride your horse at a walk and a cued trot for about fifteen minutes out in the big arena if you like. If he is not doing the things above or needs more polish on them, bring them all into play in this session. After having done or gotten through them fairly well at the end of this fourth week, we will proceed to teach him a controlled collected start using his natural or favorite lead.

After having walked around the pen to the left on the horse about four or five times, we will set him up in position for his first try to go into a smooth left lead in a gathered manner. With a rein in each hand, our hand position will be as follows: We will take the slack out of both reins. We will not be pulling but about two inches away from, where if we do pull two inches, we will then have him in the bosal in the hackamore. Our hands at this point will be positioned closer to the horse's head than we have been riding him. They will be about even with the front of your saddle, well below the horn and about even with the swell of your saddle.

As we go around this pen at a walk to our left, we will keep our horse away from the rail or fence about two feet. Now we will take up on our right rein enough to bring the horse's head to the right about eight inches to one foot out of line with his body. We will then start to squeeze the right side of this horse with the calf of our right leg, then touch him lightly with the right spur after the squeeze. Remember, squeeze first, then apply your spur. He will move away from the squeeze of the leg and the taped rowel of your spur with his hindquarters. As we are pulling his head to the right holding his front end to the right, his left shoulder will be forced out and ahead. Be watching his left shoulder. Do not put your weight on his left shoulder or lean in that direction. Put your weight on his right side. Cluck at him and work your right leg into him and touch him lightly with the right spur. You will also have the slack out of your left rein. This puts the horse into the bosal to check him. At his first attempt to bring that left shoulder up, you have to be ready to release his head with the right rein, and at the same time let him go on into a lope.

Read this over several times. Remember, it all has to go and follow together to get it done right. If he raises his shoulder but fails to go into a lope, slow to a walk then ride around a circle or two and repeat the things you just did. He will not get this right away. It's going to take him several attempts to put it together. So don't get discouraged, but keep trying.

The horse will become confused at this point. He will think first that he is supposed to stop, because you are pulling his head out to one side, but urge him on at a walk by letting him have a little slack on your inside rein. After going on two or three times like this, he will start to figure that you did not want him to stop. He will start to get the idea from the right side pressure of leg and spur that he is supposed to go on. If it becomes apparent to you after several tries at a walk that he is not attempting to do what you want him to do (that is lope), let him trot a few steps with his head pulled to the right. Then keep after him with your right leg and spur until he breaks into a canter or lope. Watch his shoulder. The left one should come up first and be sure you release his head at that split second when the shoulder comes up and he starts into the lope after a few steps trotting. Let it go on a few times. But each time check him with your reins until you have discouraged the trot. Use the same cues every time. It won't take over two or three training sessions before he will understand that it's a lope you want whenever the cues are applied. Work on this left lead until the horse is doing it real well. It may take you about ten days to get it going smoothly. As he progresses, slacken up on the angle that you pull his head to the right. When it's working well, you won't be pulling his head out of line with his body over about two inches.

The horse, when being pushed into this lead collected instead of jumping into it extended, will sometimes have his leg behind him instead of under him when he attempts to bring his shoulder up in going into the lead. So you might have to keep the pressure on your reins until he corrects himself and takes another step to bring his lead leg under him. He will figure this out in time and will eventually get himself set up to make a smooth start. So, do not attempt to slow the horse down after he has started these first few lopes. You can do it later once he has gotten the message and understands the cues of the start.

There is one other thing I'll mention here. A horse trained this way will get the habit of starting slow, and after some practice will continue to lope slow. Where the horse that goes into the lope or canter extended will have to be taught to slow down, which means you are going to have to pull him harder to get it done. When once he's used to the collected start by being pushed into the lead with a little checking with reins on his front end, he will start smoother, slower, and will likely continue at a more collected lope with less or no rein contact. Remember at the exact time that he raises his shoulder to start into the lead, your hand position, though closer to his head than in the other things you have taught him, will always remain in the down position in relation to the pull on the bosal on the bridge of his nose.

I do not put any horses I train into a training fork or running martingale or tie down, until they are reining real well. I advise you not to get in a hurry on your head set. Keep your mind directed on your pulls on your reins on either hackamore or snaffle. The pull should be even with your belt or slightly below. If you repeatedly have your horse in any head gear with your hands high, you will be training your horse's head up instead of down. If you try to teach neckreining or other subjects in a martingale prematurely, before your horse is light in the hackamore or snaffle bit, he will not have complete freedom of his neck and head to learn to do it efficiently. He cannot have this freedom of movement once he's put into a martingale, training fork, or tie down.

Because so many stops have to be made in teaching leads, the neck stop for me has been invaluable. I can stop a horse without hauling hard with my reins. You will have to stop your horse and correct him many times in his training process. So teach this neck stop to your horse. It will come in handy many times before you have a finished product. He will respond to it rather than be hauled to a stop. It can also be used later on your pleasure horse, where you can simply give your rein hand a quick drop of about two inches, and your horse will take this as a cue for a stop while you are riding with your reins set in one position in one hand. When you are within two inches in your rein slack from the animal's nose or mouth, the horse soon learns to watch those reins. If he sees more slack in them as you apply the next stop, he will soon learn that a sudden drop in the reins means a touch on the neck for a stop signal. He will already be stopping before your hand touches his neck. When he's this far in his schooling, he will take a quick two or three-inch drop in the reins as his stop signal. It works smoothly. The horse won't raise his head when he stops, whereas if you get a hold of him and pull, he will sure raise his head to some extent. The horse to remain light and improve on his reining ability should have complete head freedom, other than what pressure you put on him with your reins and hands. This is why I do not believe in putting him in a martingale before he's reining well.

I will also brief you here on what I've said about discouraging the horse from trotting while attempting to put leads from a walk into a lope. In the past we have encouraged a cued trot and have worked it a lot on him. But in trying to teach him a lope or a canter, we discourage the trot because we are trying to get lope on the horse's mind. You will find some horses will react to this after you have him well started on his correct leads from a walk to a lope. You will have to start over on the trot and make him trot. He can get a little "lope simple," but with a little patience, he will revert back to original cues and settle down, and trot. The cue for the trot or jog should be a light easy squeeze with both legs and a touch with spur. If he takes to the trot with just your leg squeezed against his sides, do not touch him with your spur. When you cue for the trot use as little leg pressure as you can. Just ease it on him. Don't use more squeeze than you have to. Do not raise or pull on your reins to get it done. You use both of your legs to cue for the trot.

You have heard the expression of working the horse and lots of wet saddle blankets. Nobody has given a definite explanation of what these subjects consist of. Let's take the phrase "Working the Horse" first. Hardly if ever, barring extremely hot July or August heat, will you wind up with a puffing, dripping horse with sweat running from him. So remember, don't think that because the animal is not hanging his head in exhaustion at the finish of the session that he has not been worked or been taught. On the contrary, it seldom occurs in the first two months of stock horse training except when running into a problem. By teaching the horse one thing at a time and gradually bringing more new things into his daily training, you will have put them together slowly. He should and will if handled right not have been hurt too much in the process. After working on any one thing or part of something new to him, you should be stopping at least every five minutes. Just sit and let him relax. Do not get on him and drill, drill, drill. He will look forward to these short stops and rests. He will accept his training more calmly. It will also be teaching the horse to stand quietly. You have, I'm sure, seen horses that will not stand still. These are the horses that have never been rewarded with frequent rests or pauses in their early training. By stopping briefly every few minutes the horse does not learn to dread the training sessions or become sour on them. I'm not saying that he should be completely dry and not sweating. He should be, but he sure should not be hurting from the work either.

As to the saying "Lots of Wet Saddle Blankets." Let us say if it's very hot weather-wise, that after an hour's work the blankets will be wet. There could be an odd horse or two that you might have to ride harder each session, but they are an exception rather than the rule. I believe once the horse is ridden to the point where he's puffing and breathing real hard, you might just ride him from that time on. I don't think you are going to teach him very much. I think you are better off to cool this horse out and start again the next day. I maintain a horse learns his best after he's just been ridden about fifteen minutes at a walk and jog trot, and that the next forty-five minutes will be when he actually learns the best. When he starts to tire, he will not do as well, nor will he learn much the first fifteen minutes out of a stall because he won't put his mind on his work.

In teaching these leads to pleasure horses, until the horse gets used to the leg squeeze on his right side, thus cuing him for a left lead, you want to make sure that you do not use your left leg to pressure him while applying the cue on the opposite side, because you will be using both legs with a gentle squeeze as a cue for a trot. You will also be using a light touch of both spurs without a squeeze for cue to start at a walk. You will give the horse some slack in the reins. In other words, move your hands forward when you cue for a walk from a stop. Then resume your original hand positions. You will also give him rein slack when you cue for this trot. Remember, the less pressure you have to use in a cue to get results, the smoother your horse is going to operate, when you do get to the collected lope. This will be the only time you will be coming back on your reins. Once the horse has learned these cues, he will know that when the rein slack comes out and the slack is held, he will be waiting for that leg pressure to follow to tell him which lead he's supposed to start in.

Let me describe what a finished pleasure horse should be doing. He will walk with a brisk walk like he is going some place. He will move into a slow smooth jog, doing both of these with reins relaxed and no contact on his mouth. Then with a light contact into the bit, he will gather up, feel the leg pressure and will answer to a light squeeze to ease into a collected start in either lead. I'm sure you have seen pleasure classes where, when a judge calls for a lope, everyone seems to duck either to the right or left depending on which lead is called for, almost as though they were all bowing to the judge. In some extreme cases, like they are about to fall on their head. A horse isn't that dumb. There's a different way. Instead of throwing all that weight on the lead legs you want him to use, it should be lightened so he can start into them easier. Then once he is started in the lead, you should try to ride him with your weight evenly distributed on him. Use your knees. Flex them to take part of the shock of the movements of the horse's gait at the same time getting into the rhythm of the horse's action by getting some weight off his loins by pressure on your stirrups. I've mentioned before, this requires that your legs be down in line with your hips. If you are pushing your boots ahead in your stirrups, you will be sitting flat down on your horse at all times. Let your legs come straight down. Do not squeeze or grip the barrel of your horse. Learn to do this relaxed.

Before going back to our lead work, at this point, let's say a few words about the walk. A horse has to be taught to walk right the same as any other gait. Up until now, we have not talked about it because we have been pretty much occupied with getting him broke and started on these various subjects. Once we have him going or at least started in these various directions, you want to start to ask yourself some questions. For instance, is my horse walking out in a businesslike way, or is he just kind of slouching along any speed he chooses to take with me? When you start out on a training session, keep it in mind. If he is not doing it right, start to improve him.

Question number two: Is he trotting slow and smooth? If not, work on it. Pull him down to the desired speed, then gradually get off your reins. If he starts to speed up again, slow him down again. When you cue for a trot use the minimum pressure to get him to trot. If you start him easy and slow, he will be more likely to continue slow. This also applies to the lope. When you are riding this horse, and he continues to want to look right or left and move his head out of position, don't wait. Straighten it out. That's all you have to do on that horse is ride him and correct mistakes. Seldom does any horse do things correctly when he first starts something that is new to him. Every time the trainer saddles a horse for a training session, he should have reviewed yesterday's results in his mind and picked out the weak points in the horse's functions. You will then work on those weak points to improve them. Then any known big mistakes, or small ones for that matter, should be attended to at once and not let it be repeated over and over again. The longer a horse goes on making a mistake the harder it is going to be to correct him. You will also have to have a general idea of what measures you are going to use to get it done.

Now back to the leads. Work this horse on his natural lead from a walk into a lope until he is working pretty good at it. Don't expect him to do it smooth at the start, but he should be doing it at the end of ten days to two weeks. When he is, you are now ready to start him on his other lead, which is his unnatural lead. Some horses are handy and there won't be much difference. But a lot of them need a lot of time and steady work to get used to it and perfect it. He will need all the patience and help you can give him.

To determine which is the horse's natural lead, watch him when he is loose in a pen. The lead he moves into when galloping will tell you which is his natural lead or the one he's accustomed to using the most. This is the lead that you will work him in first. Continue to work this lead until he is doing it well, and he is doing it with a light cue of the leg asking for that lead.

He has now accepted the fact that the cue is a signal requesting him to start promptly into the lope or canter. By doing this same thing when you start on the opposite lead, he will soon put it together that he's expected to lope by the same cue, only it's being given on the opposite side. Let's go over briefly what we did to get the horse to take his natural lead. We shortened up our rein hand position, so that we would be nearer our horse's mouth or nose. After having taken a shorter rein on our right side, and we have pulled his nose to the right, then we have pushed him with our right leg and followed up a light touch of the taped rowel of the spur. We have pushed his hindquarters to the left. In this manner we are also forcing his left shoulder out. This puts him in position to make it convenient to bring his left leg and left shoulder up to start him into a left lead lope. To work his right lead you would go the opposite direction around the pen or arena and apply the same tactics only on the opposite side. Stay a yard away from the fence so you have plenty of room to set the horse's head to one side, and freedom to work on the side of the horse with leg and spur cues. Remember, the leg you are not cuing with should not be squeezing the horse. Another thing to watch is that you check your horse to some extent with both hands low, while pushing this horse or cuing him with the leg into a lope. Try it lightly on the pull while still holding the horse's head to one side. Your inside hand will be putting tension on that rein also. After several attempts you will be able to determine how much pressure it will take. As the horse gets the message and starts to respond to your cue and hand position, slacken up on your rein pull as you develop his progress. I think that if you are not too informed or learned on leads, it might be wise for you to ask a friend who has some knowledge about leads to help you. He can stand in the center of the pen and tell you when the horse is right or wrong. This will give you an opportunity to stop your horse right away and start over. Remember, this is where that neck stop becomes important. It will sure save a lot of pulls on his nose or mouth. These training techniques in small areas call for many stops and starts even for the experienced trainers, so let's try to save the horse's mouth or nose any way we can. It will sure pay dividends later when we go to the other actions such as reining, roping, barrels, or whatever.

The horse in the process of learning these leads will sometimes raise the shoulder you want him to and upon being released to go into the lope, will be cross firing behind. It happens more often on his unnatural lead. But with patience and repetition he will iron it out on his own. He will not be comfortable while doing it wrong. He will find, by repetition, that it's in his best interest that he bring that same hind leg under him on the side he comes up on with his front leg to get them united for his own comfort.

In his unnatural lead, once you get him into it, you can advance him quicker by making him lope longer in that lead so he becomes more accustomed to using it. Use it a lot more than you use his natural lead. When he is starting to work in it well, you can go back to using both leads in your practice sessions.

At this time it is about time to think of getting this horse used to a snaffle bit. Take any kind of an old headstall with a brow band and throat latch on it. Then take a ring snaffle bit and put it on over your hackamore. Adjust it where it's just nicely resting on the corners of his mouth. Do not put any reins on this bit at this time. Let him wear it for at least a week each training session. But, and this is important, take a piece of leather lacing and tie this bit up in the following way: Secure one end of the thong to the top of one ring of the snaffle bit. Then take about three wraps around the top of the bosal so that it is just snug with the slack out. Secure the other end to the opposite ring of the snaffle bit. Make sure there is no slack between the bit and the bosal where the thong comes down from the wrap on the top of the bosal. This will allow the horse to become accustomed to carrying the bit without putting and starting him into the habit of running his tongue over the bit instead of under it. After a week to ten days of carrying it, we will not tie it up but let the weight of the bit rest on his tongue still without reins. The relationship between the bit tied up in this manner will be gone over again later when we go to the reins on the

Bit tied up to bosal

Photography by Neil Mishler, Ponca, Nebraska

snaffle instead of the hackamore. There's a connection here that should not be left out, because it will have a big influence the first two weeks we eliminate the hackamore and go to direct control of the snaffle bit on the horse.

Transition from Hackamore to Snaffle Bit

People who ride horses or are about to start to ride, as a hobby have for the most part little or no knowledge of the hackamore. Those who have tried it on horses have probably done so from reading about its use. Some have read books by authors who are experts with the hackamore. Their teaching, I think, has been beneficial to a certain group of people who were a good deal interested in becoming trainers themselves.

My first experiences with this piece of headgear put me in contact with it from necessity. While I was working for several cattle outfits, I would be given hackamore horses, ones that were broke, also snaffle bit horses that were broke, and horses that were grazing bit horses, and an occasional spade bit horse. These horses were chosen for me and not picked by me to punch cattle on. Had I had a choice I would have probably put more confidence in the grazing bit or curb bit horses. I soon learned that the real hackamore horse that was five or six years old and for whatever reason had not been bitted, surprised me in his ability. They would handle like a reining horse and would cow with the best of them. After some experience with them and knowing what they could do sold me on the idea that the hackamore was sure a good piece of headgear or how could these horses have been brought that far with it. I didn't train them, but I was convinced they didn't learn to handle the way they did by accident. One maybe, but I rode several. I never knew or saw the men that had trained them. I also knew I was going to learn its use if I ever intended to train horses.

For the inexperienced I would advise them not to figure they could go out and beat the world in one. But if the information I have furnished is followed within a controlled area and not in open country, I am sure you will produce a better, lighter, reined horse than if you went to a snaffle bit in his first schooling. I think the hackamore in inexperienced hands, in contrast to the bit in inexperienced hands, is by far the lesser of two evils. I think the hackamore will cause a horse to make less mistakes and have a tendency to spoil less horses than the bit in the first two months of his training. It is not my intention in these writings to make expert hackamore reinsmen out of you readers. But to show you who have had no experience, and you with some experience, some guidelines to get a horse started and with enough time, develop a better than average horse. Perhaps help you to the point where you just might avoid spoiling your horses. Most horses don't spoil themselve. It is accomplished for the most part by using wrong methods and failure on the owner's or trainer's part to communicate with the horse. Wrong methods have been used in the handling of him. Even if your methods are not professional and take a longer period of time to accomplish them, there is enough information here to produce a pretty good horse if followed. I have been and am writing from a trainer's experience on lots of different kinds of horses. I did not deviate from my methods described in general on any of them, with the exception of spoiled or problem horses from time to time.

I have written from my own experience in training for the public, which meant to ride all the horses I was working six days a week. I would have to lay one up occasionally for from two days to a week for lameness caused from farriers, soreness, distemper and cinch rash. Those were the main reasons that caused lay-ups. Sometimes a horse would react to a distemper shot and his neck would be too sore to allow him to work. I finally got smart enough to tell the vet to needle him in the chest or some other area. This helped in that way. I will add further that it takes a steady lick to get what we have gotten done on the horses described in the writings. To get one that far in the length of time given, you have to ride them pretty steady. You who are just starting, don't get discouraged if you don't get as much done in the specified time talked about here. Even if you take twice the time and come out with near results, you will be all right. But ride your horse as regular as you can, or as your time will allow you. Spread over a longer period of time, you might come out better than using the time I've prescribed.

Don't get in a hurry when handling your horse. If he's making a mistake, watch him closely and also your own actions. Think, think. You can probably figure the mistakes out and correct them.

Keep in mind he is a dumb animal and that you should be able to outthink him. Sometimes you have to fool him. One thing for sure, once you know he's making a mistake, think ahead of him and catch him in the act. He will almost for sure give you a clue that he is going to do it. You should use measures to counteract it at the second he does it. So try and be prepared for it.

Let's go a little further on the subject of rein hand position. You will not and cannot when you're mounted on green horses try to school him with your reins set in any one position. Because if you try it, the horse is bound to make a move that will demand you change your hand position on your reins a lot of times. What you will do is think ahead of your horse. Prior to getting a horse to make a certain move, you will set your hands accordingly, the right distance with the reins from hand to nose or snaffle. In other words, you get set up for whatever move you are trying to get the animal to do before he does it, not afterwards. A man training horses will be constantly changing rein hand position to fit the need of the moment. In watching a good trainer work a young horse, you will be amazed at the swiftness he can pick up slack with a rein in each hand. Let out the slack in one rein and take up slack with the other hand. A man with long experiences on many horses gets to be automatic at it. Ninety percent of the time he is ahead of the horse countering every move, every turn, by manipulating his hands on those reins. It becomes almost a habit.

It is now time to start writing about coming out of the hackamore that has been used on the horse. The next step is to go into snaffle bit work with him. When going to a snaffle bit on the horse for the first time with the reins on it, leave your halter on the colt. Instead of putting the hackamore on him put the snaffle bit on him. The snaffle is not a strange thing to him, because we have worn it on him over the hackamore with no reins attached to it. We have also tied it up for a week so there's been no weight on the horse's tongue from the bit. When we tie this bit up this time, we will use the nose band on the halter to tie the bit up as we did the top of the bosal. One thing you might take note of here is where the nose band on the halter sets on the horse's nose. It should set at least as high as the bosal was on his nose. This will enable you to have the bit tied up in about the right position. Once you have inspected it carefully to make sure the weight of the bit is supported by the thong you used to tie it up off his tongue is about right, you are ready to mount up. When you first start with it, you

Snaffle tied up to halter nose band and proper hand position on rein

Photography by Nell Mishler, Ponca, Nebraska

can expect some reaction, but it won't last too long. I would take a guess at about three training sessions of about forty-five minutes to one hour in length for each session.

You will at this time take it easy on your horse. Do some of the simple kind of things you first did in the hackamore such as circles clear around the breaking pen or arena. Three or four one way and that many in the other. Make some large figure eights. Going three times one way and three times in the other, then connecting up once in awhile and do a complete one. But do them at a walk or slow trot the first few sessions. Do not lope your horse in these first lessons in the snaffle. You will find that by a pull on your reins one way or the other, by having your bit tied up, it will have some hackamore effect to it. When you pull on one rein, the pull will be on the nose band on the halter with a little pressure on the horse's mouth as well. This helps a great deal in his transition from the hackamore to snaffle bit work, and it really works just that way.

You will operate the reins on this snaffle bit the same way you did with your reins on the hackamore. You will also remember to keep your hands down on each side as you did in the hackamore. Run a test on this horse occasionally with both reins in one hand. You should have been doing this while in the hackamore, too, after the first two weeks.

If the horse is operating pretty good in his neckreining when switching to the snaffle bit, he will still need a lot of work with a rein in each hand. You should have no more slack in your reins than when you put tension on your reins, your hands would move back about two inches and you are in contact with his nose or mouth. If your hands are too high and you pull back and up on your reins, your rein hands will be out of position and will be about in line with the top of your rib cage or wishbone on your chest. It looks bad at this point. You are also out of position to control your horse.

The test for neckreining with one hand holding both reins is as follows: Make sure your reins are even when applying your neck rein. Look at the horse's nose and head. When he turns in the direction you are reining, but has stuck his nose out to the right and you were neckreining to the left, even though he turns left, he's a little bit wrong. Now if he were in the hackamore, the way you would start to correct him would be, after applying the neck rein to rein left, and if he did not immediately turn his nose left and follow it; you would take the left rein in your left hand and give it a sharp tug on his nose. Then pull it left. Continue to do this until whichever way you rein, the nose is the first thing that moves in the direction you are reining. But we are now in a snaffle and you cannot snap with that inside rein to correct him without jerking his mouth. So the substitute for it is done by first taking the slack out of the rein. Then with slack out, and you have made light contact with his mouth, you will give it a quick short pull after you have laid your neck rein on his neck on the opposite side. Until the horse is doing all the things neckreining in the snaffle with two reins in one hand as well as he would do in the hackamore, he still needs some more work with a rein in each hand. If you are schooling a horse that has been started with the hackamore, and this horse gives you a problem in a given area with the snaffle bit, I strongly advise you to put this horse back into the hackamore for the period of time required to make the adjusted improvement. Then go back to the snaffle when the improvement has been made with the hackamore. By so doing you will lessen the chances of hurting the horse's mouth during the procedure.

When we are talking abut what the horse should be doing up to his lead work, he should be making the following moves: With both reins in one hand, he should walk out briskly. Go straight without turning his head one way or the other. He should be able to make those figure eights in a precise pattern at a trot. He should be able to make a half eight several times one way, then several times the other without breaking off on his own to take a different direction unless reined to do so. You will still have to help him to set him up for his leads from walk to lope or canter. This latter part will continue a long time even after he's been in a snaffle bit, because it's one of the more difficult subjects to teach the horse to do, if it's to be done right.

We have described how to run a thong down from the brow band to fasten to the centerpiece that's holding the bit up off his tongue. Until this horse is neckreining and handling fairly well, do not put him in a martingale or training fork at this time. Let's bring a few other things into focus here about neck reining. Let's go back to the third week in the hackamore. You have ridden this horse twenty-five or thirty times, and he isn't putting any effort into his neck reining. You have a choice of discipline here, either spurs that are taped or the bat. Let us say that the horse is going pretty good to the left but is sluggish reining to the right. I would go back to the breaking pen and ride this horse around slow at a walk or trot to the right. Then I would get set up for the move I was going to make to correct or improve him. Take both reins in one hand with your palm down. Have your reins placed in the palm of you hand, one rein resting against the other forming a cross in the center of your palm that is down. Either end of each rein will be on the opposite side of the horse's neck. Now adjust them so that your right rein is about six inches shorter on the side you are having the problem with the horse in turning. Start with your hand on the short rein pulling into a small circle. Then when you make this pull with the hand low and back, it will also place the neck rein against his neck on the opposite side. Give him a light pop with a bat about eight inches in front and above his shoulder at the rear of his neck at the point where the neck rein makes contact on his neck. Pull the horse into a tighter circle, then give him another pop. Put your bat back on your horn and ride around a few circles.

Then ask him again to turn lighter and easier. If he fails, repeat the lesson with the bat. If it's the other way he's failing to turn like he should, lightly and with the first contact on the neck rein, put it on him again after reversing your rein hand position. You will find that some horses with manes on them will be reining better in the direction opposite of where the mane hangs than on the side which is carrying the mane.

You want to strive all through the horse's training to even up his reining to the right and left. Another method I go to is the use of the heavy deep roper stirrup that is leather bound. With a rein in each hand, I will ask the horse to neck rein to the left and make a fairly tight circle. If he does not get into it the way he should, I'll reach up and pop him with the flat of that stirrup on his shoulder. Remember, always give him a chance to do it before resorting to these disciplinary measures. If he does not respond to either of the other mentioned measures, I'd not hesitate to spur him in the shoulder once I'm sure he knows what I want him to do. I prefer the stirrup and spur rather than the bat. If you overwork the bat, the horse gets jumpy in regard to your movements of your hands using the reins. Where with the stirrup and spur I can sometimes just threaten him with one foot or the other and get results. It also leaves my hands free to position and control my horse's head.

Let's get back to getting this horse to back up without hauling his head off with those reins in the hackamore or snaffle bit. This backing up of the horse should be confined to about two lessons per training session. I will give you my ideas on how best to accomplish it. Whatever discipline administered to the horse should never be given or put into action until we have our hands in position and have made the horse take at least one step backwards from the start. Let us say that he is going back and has been, but is not doing it very well or doing it sluggishly. After asking the horse to back, and you have pulled his nose down, and he has started back one step, raise both stirrups and pop him once on each shoulder with the flat side of the stirrup. To get this done you have to loosen up your legs, thighs, and body. Immediately after using the stirrups on his shoulder slacken up on your rein pressure each time. After he starts back take the pressure completely off your reins and don't be pulling hard. Keep backing this horse a little further every day. If he does not respond to the stirrups, use your spurs once in his shoulders until he's coming back faster and on a lighter pull. As he improves a little each day lay off the discipline.

Reward him every time he makes more effort. Now let us say that after a week of this, he is backing much better but is backing crooked. You can now straighten him out by using a spur in him on the side he's circling to. Catch him when he is first starting to back crooked. Then while keeping the spur in him lightly, pull his head in the opposite direction but keep backing him. Make him use the other hind leg. Once you know he is making an effort to back straight and he's conscious of it, take your spur out. Give him a chance to practice it on his own before going back to discipline. When he makes an effort in the right direction, reward him and stop for that session. It won't be long before you can cue for a back by just moving both feet ahead with your stirrups about three inches and with a little pressure pulling back on your reins, your horse will start back. Just the second he starts back bring your stirrups back to normal position. Be ready with your spurs to drive him on back. Be ready to correct him if he points his butt in one wrong direction or the other. Apply these things a little on every training session. Remember, don't get angry or shook up. Use patience and give the horse a chance before getting after him.

Once a horse is starting to rein fairly well, is stopping with a neck cue, is answering a cue for a trot, is loping in both leads, is making those figure eights (big ones) at a trot, and is backing pretty decent, you can think about puttng him in a running martingale. When you buy one, it will probably be made for the long-necked saddle-bred horse and of the English type. I like the over-neck strap on these in preference to the training fork. You will have to work this martingale over. The fork straps with the rings will be too long. You will have to cut them off. They should be about eight inches long from the beginning of fork to ring. The strap going to your front ring on your cinch will also be too long. I recommend that you cut part of this strap off and attach a ring to it. Then fasten a small snap to the little ring on the front of your cinch. The martingales do not come with a ring on the end of the connecting strap. The English people simply run their girth through the double portion on the end of the strap, then tighten their girth. I don't think you can run your cinch on a stock saddle through this leather loop on the end of the martingale and tighten it up without causing some discomfort to the horse. The more comfortable you can make your horse the better he will school. Your saddle shop man will probably rework the martingale for a small fee if you tell him how you want it done.

When first putting your horse into the martingale, put it on him when you start out. But do not put your reins through the rings when you first start riding him with it. Ride the horse for about thirty minutes and get him settled down. Then dismount and put your reins through the rings and get aboard. But on these first three or four sessions, don't try to do too many things. Just ride him and let him get used to this new piece of gear. The reason you would not put your reins through the rings at the start is that if the horse is high and playful, the first thing he will do is raise his head and find the rings causing a solid pull down. It's hard to tell what he might do. So introduce this piece of equipment gradually and give him time to know it's there. You are going to use this martingale as a head setting device. It's to make this horse hold his head straight while he's traveling and to get him to flex at the poll. There's a lot to learn here on the rider's part also.

Remember, we still have this bit tied up. In his first lessons most of the pressure will be on his nose and not on the bars of his mouth until he is used to carrying his head in a low flexed position. You will handle your reins with a rein in each hand just as you did before. One big difference that will occur is how much tension you will use on these reins on a straightaway or in a big circle. Put a little tension on your reins and hold the slack. As soon as the horse gives to it and lowers his nose, give him a little slack on your reins also. What you are trying to get across and will be with the martingale's use, is that when he gives by dropping his nose, you will also give slack with your hands. Remember, this is the way to get your horse to flex properly at the poll. To ride this horse with a set rein and not to give to him when he drops his nose will cause him to start to be a head bobber, even though he is carrying his head down and nose tucked; or he will freeze with his head set in one position and will not flex at the poll, because the rider failed to relax the rein pressure when the horse gave to the bit.

You should also when using the martingale, use some guards between your bit and the rings that your reins run through. You can make a pair by simply cutting two square pieces off from an old latigo about two inches square. Take your knife and make a slit in each one of these squares long enough so that you can slip a rein through each one. Push them up all the way to your rein connection on your bit. Then run your reins through your martingale rings. This will prevent your ring getting hooked on the bit or rein connection, causing your horse's head to get caught in that area and perhaps hurt his mouth. He will certainly jerk to free himself, when he finds he's tied to it. You can buy them, too, if you like. Most saddle or tack shops handle them.

We talked in some of our previous writing of tying our reins together so that we might not drop one. Some colts in your efforts to retrieve it would likely spook. However, when your horse is far enough along you can stop doing it any time you think it is safe. I also find average bridle reins in length okay for just riding, but find them too long for convenience in training. You can use them as is or cut a foot off from them if you like.

When you run a neckrein test on your horse, you do so by holding both reins in one hand. You will find that by holding your reins in one hand with your palm down and your reins crossing each other in your palm and each end of a rein is on the opposite side of the horse's neck, its use is of value. It will allow the reins not to touch either side of the horse's neck except very lightly. When you do rein him to right or left one rein goes away from his neck while the other is being placed on his neck. At the same time his head is being held in position using this method. In this way the horse has a definite feel on one side and is not being touched on the other side to confuse him. Later on it won't matter as he will get used to the feel of one rein pressure more distinctly than the other. It is simply a means of the horse being able to identify between the two. It will lessen his doubts as to what's expected of him in his early stages of neckreining.

The methods we have invoked to get him to rein have been to keep one rein away quite some distance and applying the neckrein at the same time. This is how he got the message from the beginning with a rein in each hand.

There are two distinct ways of holding the reins in the early stages of testing the horse on his neckreining. The first and the one used extensively in the early stages is the method of holding the reins crossed in the palm of the hand with the palm down. This is used to enable us not to confuse the horse in the process. This method gives the horse an opportunity to concentrate on each individual rein.

The other method is holding two reins in one hand with palm down using only the forefinger to separate the reins. This method should be used only when the horse is pretty well advanced in his neckreining training, because it does allow both reins to touch his neck. This latter method of holding the reins will be and should be the method used on the finished horse.

We will now review the last or past week in the martingale and snaffle bit. Towards the end of the week, we have taken up our leads in the last two sessions of the week with the horse in the martingale. We have taught this horse to stop by the neck stop as we were doing previously in the hackamore. We have introduced him to the lead work from walk to lope by leg pressure, touch of spur, and a little tightening of our reins to move him into the required lead. We have started these measures in the snaffle as well without the hackamore.

We can now start doing the leads with the reins through the martingale rings. From now on the martingale will also be a good piece of gear in teaching the horse more collection into the leads. It can be employed in helping him to stay more collected at the lope or canter. The horse with a short stride and the short-legged horse can lope in a straight line more slowly than can the long-legged, long-bodied horse. In trying to get a horse to lope slow, you will find it less difficult to accomplish with the short-legged, short-bodied horse because he does not have to gather up as much. His stride is short. He will naturally be covering ground at a slower rate than the other type. Neither will he have to raise his legs high off the ground to accomplish it. The rangy-type horse will have to use more collecting and raise his legs higher to take shorter steps to get the same results. But once he has learned enough collection to get it done in a straight line without moving his rear end to one side or the other, to cover the ground slower, and to shorten up his stride, and can do this on a loose contact with his mouth, this type is beautiful to watch. He will be pulled out and placed in pleasure classes by most judges in preference to the short-legged type.

The circles that you should be making in figure eights will help develop this collection. The size of these circles should be made in their initial stages about sixty feet long and split down the middle so each half of the figure eight would be about thirty by forty feet in diameter. This gives you plenty of starting room to set your horse up for a lope. Each time you have gone about three or four turns in one-half of a figure eight, cue him for a stop in the center of the eight. Give him a little breather. Then start in the opposite lead going in the opposite direction in the other circle. Make three or four circles in that lead. Stop again. Give him a short rest. Reward him. After a few days of working this into your training sessions along with the other things we have covered, you can start to make one-half of the eight. Stop your horse. Then start right out in the opposite lead and continue on the other half. In this fashion, you can get a lot of starts on leads, working cues, and reins. Do the half circles first. Then work in three or four of the figure eights without stopping long in the center. Stop just long enough that the horse has time to gather up, and you have time to readjust the reins. Then cue for the lead you want. It won't be long and he will fool proof himself from missing a lead. It is also setting him up for a flying change later on.

We are now at the point where we are going to have to watch this horse more closely. Here is what happens. In the horse's efforts to please you and being a creature of habit, he will from this point on start to anticipate some of the moves you are going to make. You are stopping for shorter periods of time before cuing and starting in the opposite lead. This works to the trainer's advantage in some things and is a disadvantage in others. One of the things that is a disadvantage is on these eights. By stopping in the center for shorter periods and starting the other direction right away, he will soon figure out this to the point where he won't wait on you for a cue. He will break off in the opposite direction on his own. To avoid this, make sure you do the half figure eights enough times and stop long enough when doing whole figure eights that he is not trying to break off on his own. Teach the horse to wait for the cue.

I have mentioned previously to get this horse used to starting in the required lead not to put your weight on it. Once he does pick up the lead, you will start to ride that lead. In other words don't get your body out of proportion by leaning too much in the direction of travel. You simply rest a little more of your body weight on the lead you are in than the other. Keep this position when riding your circles. Ride that lead right on to the time you stop this horse. He will soon get to know and feel that by the weight of your body, that is the way he is to continue to travel. Later on we will find that a shift in weight, combined with a light check on our reins, plus an opposite leg cue means go to the other lead.

You might also do these different maneuvers on your horse by choosing different ground to work on. This will acquaint him to the fact that he is expected to work wherever you might choose to ask him to do so. It will also come about in the third or fourth month of his training that he has to work in the company of other horses. Sometimes this is easy to get done and sometimes it poses a problem, depending on the disposition of the horse. We will cover this in detail later on.

Let us go back once more to what we have accomplished. If we aren't there yet, what we will be shooting at towards a finished pleasure horse for competition or just a good riding mount. The things we have done and our continued advancement should produce a mount that is capable of either, and also will be a horse, if inclined in a given direction, to show some promise as a prospect for other events such as reining, roping, trail, Western riding, and even, perhaps, cutting. All the things we are doing, plus what we will be doing, will enable this horse to go on to other things. Most trainers would be glad to take such a horse to go on into any of the events I've just mentioned. I have given you enough information and instruction that will cover the first sixty days or three months. If you have hit a steady period of riding, even though the training sessions have been limited to an hour a day of actual riding time, you will have gotten a horse to the point that I'm going to describe in the next few paragraphs.

I go over to a stall, catch my horse, take him over to the hitching spot or snub post and latch him to it. Go over to the tack room and get my tack, comb, hoof-pick, and brush. Go back to my horse. Give him a thorough brushing. Take my hoof-pick and clean his feet. Incidentally, he could have been shod after the first six weeks of training. He may need the protection the shoes can give him, as we are working the horse faster and longer. Even with no rocks, the ground gets mighty hard when you are working every day.

We then saddle up. Put on our martngale and bridle with snaffle bit tied up. Lead our horse off center and around for a couple of minutes. Reach down and get a front foot and bring it forward and then the other one. This will free any hair that might be caught in the cinch that could bother him. Then mount up. My horse should stand until I adjust my reins which at this time will not be through the rings on the martingale. I'll start out with two reins in one hand. I'll walk around the arena maybe two times one way and turn into the fence, and walk two times around it the other. Then I'll cue for a trot, retracing the path that I made at a walk. I'll then put my horse at a slow trot and do some big figure eights. Then I'll take one-half of one eight and instead of holding to the outer circle continuously, I will keep turning this horse at a trot until I've wound him down to a circle about ten feet in diameter. Here I will pause for about two minutes and just sit and let my reins hang free. Give the horse a brief breather. This done, I'll work his reverse or back up for maybe four or five times. I will at all times be watching my horse from the time I mounted until I stopped to discover any mistakes I knew he was making. If none are obvious, I will step down. Run my reins through the martingale rings. Mount up again. You might recheck your cinch at this time also. I will then proceed to put this horse in either lead at a lope around the arena two or three times. Then I would stop and breathe him again and give him a chance to relax. I will start out again and go the opposite way for two or three rounds clear around the arena. This time, however, I would stay in a canter but shorten up my circle until I was loping in a small circle about fifteen feet in diameter. I would stop the circle reduction at the first time I felt the horse was under too much pressure to keep it up.

To do these small circles, he has to gather up to accomplish them. It will also teach him to shorten his stride. It will teach him to carry weight or stay under it in a balanced manner. Then another pause, dwell or breather. If the horse, at this point, is starting to breathe hard and is breaking a pretty good sweat, I would just ride him at a walk until he had cooled down again. I would then start some half circles at a lope a few times. One way and then stop and a few times in the other. If at any time this horse needed help or was making a mistake, I would go back to a rein in each hand and repeat that part where the mistake had been made and proceed to correct it. I would also note that if the horse had made a mistake on that session on that day, I would have it on my mind for the next session. I would stress giving it more attention and perhaps leave out something that he was doing easy, and I would spend that time on the mistake.

 **14**

Finishing the Pleasure Horse

After two weeks in the ring snaffle bit and martingale, it's time to take the tie on the bit off and let the bit rest fully on the horse's tongue. This will be the first week with the bit free. Take it easy in this week's training. Ride him longer. Use your hands in the down position with a rein in each hand. Be as light on your reins as possible because this is the first time the horse has really been in the bit. Prior to this, he has had protection from the weight of the bit and has not felt it on the bars of his mouth to any extent. Start out at a nice easy walk for awhile. Make several trips clear around the arena both ways. Keep his head straight. Apply a little rein pressure. When he gives his head or nose down, give him some slack. Try to establish just the right amount of tension on those reins that you will be using when you are neckreining with two reins in one hand. Go through all your previous maneuvers with a rein in each hand. Then when you think he's going and doing his best, put both of those reins in one hand and try to imitate the same amount of slack that you were using. Do those same things, including the back, that you just did with a rein in each hand. Don't feel bad if in the process in any one of them, you found the horse has needed some help, such as missing a lead. Go right back to a rein in each hand until corrected.

Let me mention here that the only way you have complete control of a horse's head is with the rein in each hand. With two reins in one hand, he can figure out several ways to cheat on you and will, until he has had enough two-handed training that he's given up or never started to figure how he can cheat. The sole object has been to bring this horse along in his training where he will operate with two reins in one hand as good as he does with a rein in each hand.

Many people riding horses put too much emphasis on neck

reining a horse and not enough on the rest of his training and how he is doing it. They think this neck reining thing is an outstanding accomplishment. Where to the experienced, it is one of the more simple things that can be taught the horse. When you reach the point with the pleasure horse that you can take the reins lightly in one hand and from a walk, you can lay your left rein lightly on his neck, put him in the bit with leg pressure and push to the right with that left rein and a squeeze with the right leg, and he goes up with his left shoulder or right, whichever lead you want, and hits a nice collected lead easy, gently, and smoothly, you have made a lot of progress. Then he's given a little slack in the reins once he starts into the required lead. Then he maintains that even, flowing lope two or three times around the arena. He will stop with a light shake or drop of those reins transisted from the neck stop. Then pull up to that inspection line for the judge. When he is signaled for a back, the horse will come on back with nose tucked, mouth closed, and in a straight line. Then chug right on back briskly without faltering; this horse is ready for tough competition.

One other thing, you remember all those small circles you made from a walk into a lope in each lead. The judge is liable to ask you (if you made the cut) to make one of these little circles in either right or left lead. Walk your horse out about two steps the way you are to go and put him gently in that bit. Gently stick that leg into him. Raise him smoothly into the lead required. Make a nice circle and come back to the line. You'll still be in there. It will eliminate several other horses at this point. One time I had five horses I had trained for pleasure in a class of forty-five. They took four places out of six. Second and sixth places were the only ones they didn't take. I was not mounted on any of them. It made me feel a little proud of my success as a trrainer.

Let's go back to our pleasure horse and assume he's had six weeks in a ring snaffle or dee ring snaffle bit, and also has a pretty good head set. We can now take him out, saddle him, and do all those things that pertain to a pleasure class with him. That means we will not have to use the martingale on a steady basis. The horse has a fixed jog trot and can be urged into an extended trot, then brought down to the fixed jog. This extended trot should be put on him only after the fixed slow jog has been pretty well established each time he's ridden. It will take the rein in each hand method to accomplish it. He will also at this time, when urged to extend his trot, try to lope or canter before he will extend it. The first thing you will have to do is to discourage the lope and put the fast or extended trot on his mind. Stop cuing the horse for the slow jog and use both legs to cue him for the extended trot. Do not pull up or back on your reins at this time, only enough to keep him from loping, since a pull on the reins prior to a one leg cue has meant that he is to go into a right or left lead. It will take several training sessions to get this across to him. But it is not hard to teach. Most of the time judges in Western classes don't call for it as much as they do in English classes. But you best be prepared for it. I'll add here that any horse that has been trained by the methods that I have given you in this book will work English also. I don't think any horse that I have trained for Western pleasure classes that had potential or talent in that direction would not be able, after a week's introduction to the English tack, be a horse which would do well in the English classes. They will do equally well in either. They will have to get used to the posting, but when they are far enough along in their schooling, they will in a short time adjust to the small difference.

Coming out of the ring snaffle to a shanked snaffle is your next bitting job. You can buy the lightweight, flat shanked snaffle at your saddle or tack shop. I strongly suggest its use before going to a grazing low or high port bit. You will find on this flat shanked snaffle that it has an extra slot just below where the chin strap goes under the horse's chin. This extra slot is for the purpose of four reining your horse. It's okay, if you can handle four reins. I'll give you a shortcut to it that worked pretty well for me. Take the ends of a pair of reins. Cut the three loops off that are used to secure the reins to the bottom of the shank. Then split these reins at the ends. Cut them back about six inches forming a Y or fork on each rein. Make sure the cut is identical in length. Then take one part of this split rein and attach it to the slot on the shanked snaffle. But make this part of the split rein one-half inch shorter than the one that you attach to the bottom of the shank on the bit. Attach the other rein exactly like you did the first. Take a leather punch (using the bigger hole in the punch) to punch two holes so that you can use a piece of leather lacing through the holes to secure the forked ends to the shanked snaffle bit. Then in your first use of this bit use a leather chin strap rather than the chain type. Once he is working well and is used to the new bit you can change to the chain-type chin strap if you like. Here again I would tie this bit up off his tongue for at least three sessions. By using this fork in the end of your reins, you will find that you will get less curb chain pressure which will be new to the horse. Give him time to adjust to it. The other advantage will be on the light pull. It will affect his mouth almost like the ring snaffle. A harder pull will bring on the curb chain or strap action. You can also use the martingale with this piece of gear. In introducing it to the horse, remember we have changed from the ring snaffle to a shank snaffle bit and that there will be more pressure applied to the horse's mouth, along with the use of the martingale than the horse would feel if he were in just the ring snaffle and martingale. Care must be taken in its first use because of the leverage caused by the shanks on the bit.

You can also use this rig with one rein in each hand to proceed with your horse's training. I have used this shanked snaffle bit coming out of the hackamore on many horses. But I advise you to use the ring snaffle bit first, then graduate him to the shanked snaffle bit. Some of these shanked snaffles have a tendency to pinch at the swivel attached to the side of the mouth. Cut two pieces of round latigo leather about the size of a silver dollar. Take your leather punch and punch out a hole in the center of the circle about the same size as the mouthpiece on the bit. Then make one cut to the center with your knife. Punch two holes on either side of the cut. Place it on the bit, then lace this cut together with a small piece of lacing leather. You can also buy mouth guards at your tack shop. You want to put guards on your reins between your martingale rings and the fork you have attached to your bit that is the substitute for four reining your horse. The things we have mentioned here are all pointed towards not hurting this horse's mouth and to bring him along in his training. The final end in sight is to have control on a light rein but not have to haul his mouth to get him to function. This, incidentally, is the outfit I use on horses for a lead change behind, with or without a martingale. I may alternate the martingale's use depending on what I ran into with the individual horse. I would for sure have a rein in each hand.

One thing I'll remind you of again in running into a problem with a horse in any stage of his training, don't hesitate to go back to that rein in each hand. Use the bit that is the least severe on the horse's mouth to correct the problem. There is the old saying, "If he doesn't do what I want him to do, I just go down and buy a longer-shanked, higher port bit." Don't believe it. I wouldn't put much faith in the saying.

We have taken protective measures throughout these writings to keep a good mouth on this horse in training. I cannot stress it enough. It's the number one. "Communication from Hand to Mouth." It is also valuable to keep a horse's head in at least a level position and has started him to using his head in the correct position. The guards on the bit and the guards between rein and martingale have all contributed to it.

We have now wrapped up about the ways and means on the pleasure horse prior to competition. If this horse was in a trainer's stable, I would strongly advise you to take all the necessary lessons under this trainer. This will assure you how this horse operates. There is one other thing we can touch on here. If the horse has not been ridden in the company of other horses and riders, it might be to your advantage to ask the trainer to do it. But if you have schooled your own, pick out three or four friends who have pretty solid horses that are not cranky or biting horses and ride your horse among these horses. His attention to these other horses at first will no doubt have an effect on him and cause him to make some mistakes. So keep working this horse with a group until he has accepted them and has focused his attention back to you where it belongs. For sure it's better at home than at a show where it will no doubt affect his chances to win or place. The commotion around a horse the first time he's hauled to a show usually has an adverse effect on him, although he works good at home. This should not give you a bad opinion of him, whether you are riding him or have a paid trainer on him. It will take considerable seasoning to make a horse a winner.

In our final discussions about the pleasure horse, the forked end on the reins will not be allowed to be used showing the horse. So after three sessions with the bit tied up on the shank snaffle, you can then let it down on his tongue and bars of his mouth. Go on with the split fork and martingale for about a week. Then take the fork off and start to use just the reins secured to the bottom of the shank on the bit. Here again you will take and use all the lightness in handling your reins that you can. He will react to the full contact with the bit and its all-out action on the curb strap. Do not use your martingale in your first sessions with it. Take your time at this point. Use a light rein. After three or four sessions try it with the martingale. Then alternate with it when needed. In winding up the pleasure horse writing, remember, when you want a left lead, lay your left neckrein on his neck. Then come back lightly on your reins at the same time using your right leg to cue or push him into the left lead. He should respond by gathering up, raise his left shoulder and go into his left lead. For a right lead you reverse the process. Lay your right rein against his neck. Check him a little with the bit. At the same time start putting the calf of your left leg into his side followed, perhaps, with the touch of the spurs. He should gather up and come up with his right shoulder into the lead.

Supposing you are training a horse of your own or are helping a friend with a horse, and you were trying to make a prospective pleasure horse out of him for competition. First of all you should get a professional opinion after sixty days' work on him whether or not the horse has the qualities that point towards him being a winning pleasure horse. Then you find the answer is no. The work you have put on this horse has for sure not been wasted. All the things you have done if following the past instructions and directive guidelines are the makings of the horse in any other events you might want to school him for. All horses do not make winning pleasure horses. All top pleasure horses do not make reining horses, or barrel horses, or rope horses or cutting horses. If the horse is honest, tries hard, and schools well, this type of horse may very well be suited to do some of the other above-mentioned events. At least he will turn out to be a more capable, better, pleasurable horse for just a riding horse. So although you may be disappointed in his competitive pleasure horse ability, at least you have a good broke horse that handles better than just an ordinary broke horse. If he has shown no bad tendencies, he will be worth a pretty good price for somebody who is looking for a prospect for a pleasure horse for just ordinary riding.

I have advised people about a horse I was working for them after two months' training, that he would not make it as a competitive pleasure horse. They insisted that I go on with the horse. Once in a great while I'd be wrong in my opinion, but ninety percent of the time I'd be right. If I had had a choice I would have sent him home at the end of sixty days. I would have taken the horse back a year later to rein or rope or barrel, if I thought he would make it.

There comes a point in training on any horse's schooling when he will show you what he's capable of doing. How good he would be at doing it, only the person who really knows the horse can judge him at this time. There will be things in the pleasure training he will do well and other things that he will have to do well and he doesn't or won't do well. This is enough to eliminate him in front of a judge. To hope they won't see it would be beyond the stretch of anybody's imagination. So use your head. There is a time to stop. When it's a two-year-old that is being trained, and he isn't working out as a performance pleasure horse, and the fact you can't rope, rein, or barrel a two-year-old, think in the following terms or options. Take the horse home. Ride him right. Then wait till he is a three-year-old before starting him in the other mentioned areas of training. Try to keep whatever amount of training on the horse as it is. If he has been in a professional trainer's hands, take lessons from the trainer for at least two weeks until you know how the horse works. Then ride him. You will have protected your training money invested in your horse, and if you wanted to sell the horse, you would also know how to show the horse to the best of his advantage.

Riding the pleasure horse for people who are fair riders is not too big of a job. When you get on a reining horse, you will find the situation changes drastically. You have to be a good rider, know what you are doing, know your horse, and be able at all times to help him. Riding barrel horses doesn't require the knowledge as does the person mounted on a reining horse. Roping probably takes more knowledge on a trainer's part than all the others with the exception of the cutting horse. These top cutting horse trainers are a breed by themselves in my opinion.

From a trainer's point of view, were I to start a horse and bring him up to the point where I was going on with him in his third year, in reining, barrels, roping, and even cutting, I would do all the things with him that I did from the start in these previous writings before I started training for any other event. I'd probably keep riding him and add a little more to sharpening up his reining, improve his stop, and reverse. A two-year-old can't stand the strain called for in reining, barrels, roping, or cutting.

When you do want to start this horse on one of these events you will sure be glad you brought him that far. If taken to a trainer, he will certainly be happy that he does not have to entirely remake the horse. If the horse shows a lot of quick getaway and speed and seems a little too high for a pleasure horse, but handles quiet and is gentle, he definitely would be classified as a reining, rope barrel, or pole prospect. He will have to have a good rein on him and some reining training before I'd put him on barrels. If he were mine, I would also want a flying change of leads on him. I don't mean where he will use it only in the center of a figure eight, but will change any time I cued him for the change.

Starting the Reining Horse

Prior to starting a horse on reining training, the horse's previous schooling up to this point would have been almost identical as was the training of the pleasure horse. Care was taken to start him right, to put a good light neckrein on him, and a good straight reverse. Work had been done on his right and left lead, so that he could identify them. He had been taught some collection in travel. These things were taught to the horse as a two-year-old.

Now let us assume we have a horse that has been brought along this far and he is a three-year-old. We found him to be versatile in his movements and capable in his handling. He has good withers, eye appeal, and weighs about a thousand to eleven hundred pounds. He was not a jumpy or spooky horse. That he was not a short-legged-type horse. He was carrying some muscle in the gaskin inside and outside of his hind leg. He was pretty well V'd up on the chest. He had pretty straight legs and was not sickled hocked. But had a short hock with his legs sitting a little under from the hock down. This, in my opinion, is what I would be looking for in a reining horse prospect. I would have no objection to the sex of the horse, as long as he or she was sound and not spoiled.

If this horse was brought back to me, and I had started him as a two-year-old, I would spend the first two weeks going back over the things I had taught him in his previous pleasure training. I would have figured I'd have put three to four months on him and would figure another three to four months on him before he was ready to compete in Jr. reining. If I had not started him, but he was broke pretty good, I would have to spend at least two months on him to get him up to the point where I could put a change of leads on him. I would also in that time have to sharpen up his reining, put a neck stop on him. If I did not start him, I'd probably have to build some kind of a mouth on him. But what I'm going to do in the following writing is to assume he's a three or four-year-old and I had started him and trained him.

I'm going on with this horse and describing my way of training as though I had taken up where I left off from his first earlier schooling as a greenie to the time I had him going real good as a pleasure horse. I would also prefer a horse that was not too short or thick in the neck. The thick neck in a lot of horses is a handicap in producing a light-reined horse. But it's not always proven out that way one hundred percent as far as a horse's handling ability. I've seen short-necked and pretty thick-necked horses have unusually good ability to do any thing required of them. So here we are about to start a reining horse. Having put a lot of schooling in that direction on the horse, we have covered a lot of ground in so doing.

I'm going to brief you as to what I'll expect this horse to be doing when I've finished him, at least up to the point where I think I can win a junior reining class or place him in a class A show. Let us start with the reining patterns. We will best forget about them for awhile, but keep in mind each move he will have to make to compete successfully in any one of them. If I were a novice I would, while training this horse, use another horse to go through each one until I'd memorized every one of these patterns, to the point where I was so thoroughly familiar with them that I would know each and every one of them without having to hesitate to think of the next move I was going to make. Because I would expect my horse that I'm training to be able to do in any place, at any spot, any move the patterns required. But never put them all together. Then only enough to acquaint him of a follow-through of the pattern without hesitation and without him anticipating what he is going to do next. One of the hardest things to keep the reining horse from doing is his tendency to learn how to cheat. It is up to the trainer to never let him reach that point. Many reining horses work real well for a year or two, then you don't see them any more, because they learn to anticipate moves even if only used on patterns at horse shows.

I will emphasize that the flying change of leads behind is the secret of the top reining horse. I would put his stop style second. I think also they are the hardest thing to teach a horse to do right. The man or woman riding the reining horse has to have complete control of these changes of leads to set the horse up and position him for the many maneuvers, whether it be a roll back, three sixty degree turns or pivots, or for that matter his stop. If a horse stops and slides better in a left lead than he does in a right lead, then that is the lead he should be in when making the stop that the judge is going to score him on. Stops are hard to put on a horse and great pains have to be taken that they are not overdone by too much practice. The leads are hard to put on him also, but the horse does not mind them as much in his training as he does the hard stop. If the rider knows where those hind legs are and can make sure the horse is in the lead that he needs to make a certain turn or move, the horse soon gains confidence in his ability to do it. But if he is not in the correct lead behind, he cannot make the move right, though he may flounder through it. If the horse is out of position when attempting them, it will soon discourage him where he hates to rein, especially if having to be forced into these out of position maneuvers. This prompts him to try to make it easy on himself when he is doing it wrong. This causes him to figure out little ways he can cheat to do it. Therefore, every move the reining horse makes correctly and he's in or can be changed to the position that makes it convenient for him to do it, encourages the horse to do it because he can do it easy or at least much easier than if he is in the wrong position. I thought before we actually got into training the reining horse, that if the reader has not thought about these things before attempting to ride a reining horse, it might be to his or her advantage to study the subject to some extent. If he hasn't done much thinking about it and runs into some major problems with his reining horse, he might go back to this page and description and help him find a solution to part of it. When a horse makes a good roll back on one end and fails to do a good one on the other end, you can almost figure he was in position on the first one and was in an incorrect position to make the second roll back.

Let us start on the flying change of leads. There are two ways a horse does this. Probably the one used most and what most people think is the easiest to teach a horse is as follows. The rider reins the horse over to the right or left into the opposite lead from which the horse has been traveling. The horse changes his front lead. At this point the horse is expected to change or pick up the hind lead to coordinate the movement. Now it's easy to rein the horse over into a front right or left lead. To get the horse to pick up that hind lead change is a different matter. They get it done eventually. In so doing the horse gets to thinking and knowing that in order for him to make sure he doesn't miss the hind lead, he has to go faster and faster to make sure he picks it up. It isn't long before you have a charging horse that is about half controlled and half runaway. This horse also does not wait for a cue. He chooses his own spot to execute this change of leads behind. This will cause him to foul up in some reining patterns and score him lower with a judge, perhaps so bad that the judge won't take a second look.

The other method is to get this horse to change his hind lead prior to changing in front. Perhaps this sounds more complicated to you readers than the first method. I have never thought it was. In fact, you can exercise more control over the horse using it by far than you can the first method. Another important thing, he can execute a flying change behind using the hind change first and do it slower. Where, when he is going to be reined over in front first and follow up with the hind change (picking it up), he has to be going faster to achieve it. He will also have to be going much faster to get it done in the earlier training of the flying change of leads. So he learns to get a little more out of control. It is harder for him to level off for his next action whatever it may be. Where with the change being made behind, first this horse, when finding how easy it is, gets very good at doing it. When the hind legs are off the ground, he reverses his hind leg position at this split second. He then comes down and is reined over in front and is in the correct lead. He can do this at almost canter speed. He can execute it on cue anyplace you choose to make or ask him to do it.

I'm not saying it is the easiest thing to teach a horse. Once accomplished you are never in doubt as to whether he did change behind or not. The movement is easy to feel by the rider when the horse shifts behind. While some horses that are pretty smooth at cross firing can fool a lot of people who are riding them, they are not quite sure whether he did or did not pick up the lead when reined over in front first. This causes the rider to go on and not being sure about that lead change, he will not stop the horse in his training when he should be stopped and corrected. Once this horse is accustomed to not being stopped at this point, he will go on making the mistakes over and over.

Let us now talk about what this horse will need extra in the way of equipment. He should have shoes on. Later when this horse has started to set down and slide, we will put a pair of reining slide shoes on him. It won't be until we have taught him roll backs, three sixty degree turns, and a solid change of leads behind. In learning these he has to have some pretty sure footing. The reining rear wide plates will interfere with these parts of his training. What I like to do with his rear feet is to take an old used pair of shoes that are not worn too thin, but where the toes from use have been worn off. These shoes help the horse get his hind legs under him easier when learning to stop.

You will also have to get a pair of skid boots, like ropers use on their rope horses. Get those that are made out of all leather and no elastic on the sides to join them together. I would also get a pair of boots for his front legs, because in his efforts to stop and turn sharp and wheel, he could clip his front leg with a back shoe or with either front one.

We will also be using the ring snaffle bit part of the time. Then switch to the flat shanked snaffle bit. Then in the final stages of his training go to a high port bit with swept back shanks. We have talked about the two snaffles so we'll talk about the others later.

The first thing we are going to teach this horse is a flying change of leads. In our previous training, we have discussed the big figure eights, little figure eights and how we stopped this horse in the center with a neck stop. How we could start from a stop to a canter in either lead after a short pause. We could also circle this horse three or four times in one direction without his breaking off on his own to go the opposite way until we reined him in that direction. We will put this horse back in a ring snaffle bit for his first lessons on lead changes. Do not use the martingale at this time, because here again we want the horse to have complete head freedom until we have him doing and understanding the lead changes. We will also have a rein in each hand and have the bit tied up with a chain curb strap over his nose. We are going to be stopping him a lot to correct him. These two methods are again being used to preserve his mouth. When we use the wide chin strap made of chain over his nose, a good part of any pull we make on those reins is going to put most of the pressure on his nose rather than on the bars of his mouth. By holding our hands down a little, we will try to train him with his head lowered as much as possible, which we have been careful to adhere to throughout his basic training.

From here on out we will not be trotting this horse but very little in his training. As in his reining competition training, there is no place called for him to trot. You can, however, do a little of it in warm-up sessions prior to starting at a lope in his actual training for reining. In other words, the first few minutes getting the horse's muscles limbered up, trot and lope around the arena a few times slow before going right into the more hard work which is to follow. Then sit awhile before going right into teaching him on his leads. One important thing in training this horse is that he stand still at certain times. The best way to accomplish this part of his schooling is plenty of stops and set with a slack rein. Because the more expectant this horse becomes of the faster moves he must make, the more he will try to stay ready and has a reluctance to relax unless taught to do so from the start. This is why it is so much more complicated and takes longer and more ability on the trainer's part to turn out a smooth solid reining horse. The most common mistake average people make in trying to turn out a good reining horse is they try to do too much with the horse in too short of a time.

For this reining training, you are going to have to have plenty of room. I'd suggest that the area used be at least one hundred fifty to two hundred feet long and at least fifty to sixty feet wide. The condition of the ground for the horse's footing is also important. Trying to school him on hard, dry rocky ground should be avoided. He will soon sore up. Sometimes it won't be obvious to the rider and he will misjudge the horse, thinking he is not trying, when in fact he is hurting to the point he's reacting.

If you are working outside, there should be a two-inch mulch on level ground with care being taken that rocks have been removed. You should also be careful that there aren't some rocks just below the surface of the mulch that are big and flat, and you won't know it when you hit one. If you are in an inside arena, it will probably be sand or sawdust. It should not be over three inches deep. A little less is better. The horse should have some kind of cushion to work on. This applies to all horses doing any kind of schooling. The condition of the ground he works on can help him or hurt him. Sometimes it can be bad enough to injure one seriously. You could get by on just teaching the horse a change of leads in a smaller area, but you're asking for trouble in trying to teach a horse good stops in a short area. You have got to have enough room to make a choice as to where you are going to stop and be able to let the horse run out.

Flying Change of Leads

Before we begin the actual instructions of the flying lead change, we'll outline the procedures in getting it done. We'll go back to the pleasure horse training in the area where we foolproofed the horse on his leads from a walk to a lope by going in fairly large circles and by stopping in the center of the eight. Then as soon as the stop was completed, cued the horse for the opposite lead and went on around to complete the figure eight. Once the horse had this solid in his mind, it was a simple procedure by reversing our leg cues and gathering him up with our reins to start him in the other lead.

We are going to use this same procedure in our flying hind lead changes but alter it somewhat. The rider should be aware that the horse has done enough figure eights that he is anticipating stopping in the center and going on in the opposite lead to complete the eight. The alteration we're going to make at this point is that we are only going to use one-half of the figure eight to introduce this horse to his first flying lead change.

Assuming this horse is a natural left lead horse, we will cue him for a right lead going to the right. We make a half circle and as we come to the center of the figure eight (when we're in a straight line coming down the center) we will cue this horse for the left lead flying change at the same time as we use our leg cue and spur, we will come back on our reins. Put the horse in the bit to check him. While this is taking place, we will raise up off the loins of our horse. When the lead change takes place, and we feel it, we will then shift our weight slightly to that lead that was called for in the change. But not before the lead change occurs, as too much weight shift would hinder the horse from making the change.

For clarification of using this one-half figure eight to school this horse instead of the complete eight will be as follows: We only intend to school this horse on one change of leads at a time, until he has learned that one lead change and is doing it well. To get this done using the one-half circle, we will start the same direction every time we ask the horse to make the one lead change. Then after he has made the lead change, we'll gallop on a straight line for about seventy-five feet. Then stop our horse, but if the horse did not successfully make the lead change, we would stop the horse at the exact time the mistake was made. In either case, whether he was successful or not, we would go back to the original starting point of the one-half of the figure eight or circle and repeat the same procedure. This will enable us to work on this one lead without confusing the horse by trying to teach him both at the same time.

The hind lead change that is the easiest for the horse to make, in the early stages of his training, is on his natural lead. It is easier for the horse if you start this flying change of leads by starting the horse in his unnatural lead, then switch to the natural lead. This should be done by working him in this particular change until he is doing it well. In a flying change of leads if we ask him to switch from his natural lead to his unnatural lead he will, no doubt, miss it repeatedly. At this point it is awkward for the horse to make these flying changes of leads at all. So to encourage the horse in this direction and strive to get our meaning across to him, I have found that faster progress can be made by teaching the horse to go from his unnatural to his natural lead and keep working on it until he has achieved it fairly well, before starting him on this other flying change of natural to unnatural lead. To get this done you are going to have to work on this one lead change repeatedly and avoid confusing the horse by introducing both of them to him at the same time.

Let's go over this one more time. We have made enough figure eights without splitting them up where the horse expects and anticipates going in the opposite direction and is already wanting to bend in that direction, but instead of letting him turn over and switch leads in front, we rein him away from the direction he's trying to go. We do this with a steady right neckrein against his neck and a pull to the left on your left rein with one left hand. We also have this horse in the bit, while we apply leg pressure to the opposite side of the lead we want him to take. Then wait for the feel of his change behind. The split second we feel this, we release his head and rein him over to his right lead in front. Proceed on around if the horse made the switch. Stop him down away from where he made the change and reward him.

Let me make a point clear here. The procedure we've just described in setting this horse up for this first change of leads should be repeated until such time that he has successfully made the change from unnatural to natural lead and is doing it four out of five times. After having completed a correct change of leads, let the horse lope on down for about seventy-five feet. Stop and reward him. If the horse has not been successful in completing the change correctly, stop the horse immediately. Do not discipline him except by voice. Bawl him out just a bit. We will now go back and repeat the same process over again. We will continue this pattern until he has accomplished the correct lead change before attempting to teach him the opposite change of leads. If we scold the horse at the exact time he's made the incorrect lead change, we will have been instrumental in causing him to focus more attention on it. I will stress, this is very important.

If you are inexperienced, get somebody that knows leads to watch you and help you. I think a month's work on his leads to get him started on them would not have been too much time to expect him to get this done. Don't work on these leads over forty minutes per day. But this does not prevent you from working him on his back-ups and other work he is learning. The reason I'm stressing the lead changes prior to roll backs and three hundred sixty degree turns is I believe once the horse can handle his lead changes, he learns the other more readily. It's one of the more complicated things the horse has to do. If done right, it makes him understand that those hind legs and their position makes his other maneuvers easier to do. Trainers might disagree with me on this point, but it worked the best for me. Once the horse has learned to change leads by changing his hind leads first, then I go on to other things. At the beginning, he will be going faster at the earlier part of his training in these changes. Once he has mastered them, he can do it much slower than he can by reining over into the front lead first and picking up the hind lead. Once schooled with this method, there is no reason why he should ever miss a hind lead, as he doesn't change until cued for the change. Let us add a little more to this. As you come across the center of this flat figure eight, any time you start on the straight line down the center, you can start gathering up on your reins and start cuing for that change of leads with your right leg and spur. He is already anticipating going to the left lead from the right lead and he has a pretty good distance to accomplish it in.

What you will be doing eventually as the horse starts to get these leads is be reining slightly out of the turn while you are cuing him to keep him from reining over into his right or left lead in front and waiting for that lead change behind. It happens in a split second, so you have to be ready to get off the bit as soon as you feel this change behind. When you have this horse hitting four out of five on both leads, you should start to change the horse back again and getting him over anticipating on his own to making the complete eights in linking them together. You can do this by starting to make three circles one way, then two or three the other. After about two weeks' training on these leads as I have described, run a test on the horse by going down in a straight line. Start in either lead, but know for sure what lead he is in. Then start at an angle off center using the lead he is in. Then reining a little away from the direction you are going to take, gather him up by coming back on your reins and cue the horse to the opposite lead from what he started out in. Then go at a diagonal that way and cue him for the opposite lead. When you can go down the length of one hundred fifty feet and get in about six lead changes on cue, you are making a lot of progress. Remember to get your weight off his rear quarters to help him make the flying change in the air. As he comes down he will take one step and change leads in front.

If you are having trouble putting this all together, use two reins in one hand. Take one hand to hold onto the front of your saddle for support in getting off his loin. You raise up just at the time you ask or cue for the lead change. It won't be easy. Hang in there and you'll do okay. It's hard for the inexperienced to get with all these different positions and put them together. If you think ahead of what you are going to do and at the same time try to determine what the horse does and is doing, you can work it out. You may have a bad day and want to shoot your horse, but you will be surprised at the improvement the horse makes the next day. Many times I've worked on some certain point on a horse's training, and at the end of the workout when I quit, I felt that I had not got a thing through the old pony's skull. The very next day he would surprise me by doing it almost perfect. Whether they think about it in their stall overnight I don't know and never will. Anybody that's worked a lot on horses will back me up on this. Another thing that's good for a horse that's been trained pretty steady and doesn't seem to be learning as fast as he should is a lay-up for a couple of days. Make sure he gets out in a pen for exercise each day. You will be surprised at the renewed interest he will take in his work, when you start to go with him again.

There is one reining pattern that can be used and is kind of made to order. It's the number two pattern. It calls for two circles to the right and two to the left. You can make as many circles as you like in either lead before changing him to the other lead. I use the above part of the pattern extensively once I get leads on the horse, to break and correct his anticipation, and to wait on me for cues. We will get into these roll backs later, but will not connect them up with the pattern until he's doing everything he has to do in reining. We will do each one separately to keep this horse from anticipating his next move.

The other thing that we want to get through his head is that when we want to make one of these moves, we expect that he do it anywhere, and any one individual part, or hook them all together and follow through with them. We will only hang them all together now and again and not enough so that he knows any one pattern. To you readers this would seem that you would do the exact opposite. So let me tell you, don't believe it. You will wind up with a cheating, scotching horse, and probably one of the prancy type that won't stand still. When I relax a horse and just let him set, I give him a lot of slack in my reins and relax my body when on him. It doesn't take him long to know that if there is a lot of rein hanging and I'm sitting quiet, and my legs are loose on him, that we don't plan on any moves. Don't fool him on this point.

In a short review about the flying change of leads, I would stress the use of a ring snaffle, a D ring snaffle, or a shanked snaffle. If the later doesn't work, go to the D ring snaffle. The martingale is not used on this horse on these lead changes or pivots or roll backs, three sixty degree turns or stops, until such time as the horse has advanced to the point where he's doing them all fairly well. I would also mention that he be introduced to the first use of the martingale with the ring snaffle or D ring snaffle than graduate to a shank bit later. The reason I'm stressing not using the martingale while the horse is in the process of learning these maneuvers, I believe the horse must have freedom of his head and neck to learn them. Any hindrance in that direction will only lengthen the time it takes to teach him. It would also affect his ability to go through that period of training and emerge when the training was completed with a lighter rein and mouth. Once taught, the martingale could then be used in improving on them.

After having used the one circle or one-half of a figure eight to school the horse on each individual flying lead change, and if I felt he was fairly well along in doing them successfully, I would try the two lead changes on a full figure eight. Just as a trial for the horse. At the point where the horse was doing them, let us say three figure eights out of four, without missing a lead, I'd then stop them and rarely do one complete eight at all. It is at this point you would change the horse back to making two or three circles one way, then switching leads using the flying change and proceed in the other direction making two or three circles. The horse has to be changed back and discouraged from wanting to or anticipating completing a full figure eight. He has to be taught to wait on a cue at all times by the rider. If not, this is the beginning of his being spoiled if he is allowed to continue choosing his own pattern of travel. So use your head while you are teaching this horse a lot of these maneuvers. He will work better to accomplish them with rein control only, then he will with too much restraint with a too severe bit and martingale.

 **17**

Pivots

Few people riding horses in this day and age have the privilege of experiencing the pleasure of riding a mount that will handle as the true reining horse does. One of the main reasons is that it takes a long period of time to train such a horse. Few people are capable of training one, because they do not have the knowledge and are not good enough riders to ride them. The difference in their handling could be judged as the difference between the old-style car and the modern car with disc brakes and power steering. I think as time goes on and more people get better at riding and understanding horses, the demand for these handling horses will also increase.

Even though a horse is never shown at a horse show, this same horse that has the ability to do all the things the reining horse can do would sure be a pleasure for anybody to ride for a hobby, once he has felt and seen the difference in a just broke horse and a highly trained animal. I thought I'd made these comments before starting this writing on pivots, as it is one of the things included in the horse's handling requirements.

To teach a horse to pivot, I do this from a walk, then a stop and a quarter turn. If I use an arena fence, I want the fence to be high enough so that the horse can't get his head or chin over it. Then I'll start down this fence at a walk. A wall makes a good spot to start him on this also. I'll go down the wall or fence and turn into the wall. While I'm turning the horse I'll continue to demand faster and faster turns against this wall until he is getting back on his hindquarters and coming around off the ground in front. While riding close to the wall or fence, as the horse is being turned directly into the wall, he is forced back on his hindquarters and by the weight being taken off the front of his body, he can make the turn, which will be a one hundred eighty-degree turn. Preparatory to the turn as we approach the spot where we're going to make the turn, we will use a cue. This cue consists of putting that leg which is next to the fence into the horse's belly with a hugging motion. You can also rest your taped rowel of your spur against the same side. After starting this cue you follow through with your hands by laying the neck rein against his neck lightly. Then the hand controlling the rein next to the wall or fence will pull the horse into the turn. After the turn is made, walk, trot, or lope down the wall. Repeat the procedure that you have just carried out.

If the horse shows reluctance during this procedure and does not want to make this turn fast, you may have to carry a bat. Use it on the outside of the turn to get it done, but you can also use the flat of that stirrup or spur on the outside of the turn to induce him to do it. You will do this each training session until this horse is making these turns light and consistent. The reason we have hugged this horse with our inside leg and spur prior to the turn and the outside stirrup on the turn against his shoulder is because this is one of the same procedures we will use to get this horse to pivot while standing in one spot away from the fence or wall. The inside leg will represent a holding action on one hind leg or the other of the horse as the way he is going to be taught to pivot later.

If the horse is neckreining sharp during this procedure, I'll have both reins in one hand. If not, I'll have a rein in each hand. If I have them in one hand, I'll use the other hand on the fork of the saddle to help position my body to help the horse in making these turns. This will also help you use your legs more freely. Remember, you are training a horse. You do what you have to do to get it done and forget about how you look.

It will take you about a week's work on this wall to get this horse coming around and getting back on his rear. This can be worked in with your changes of leads or during the same session. Remember, the first cue the horse has that you want a short turn is the leg and spur in his side at the same time he feels the neckrein telling him to turn into that leg. The next thing he sees is the threat of that stirrup towards his shoulder. Work him both ways alternating your leg position for each turn. It won't be long before he gets the message. You can also use a bat for this purpose, if you are one handing the horse. When he makes the first move to come off the ground in front to make that turn, stop and reward him with voice and touch. Repeat it after letting him rest awhile. It won't be long before he is doing it both ways. Now quit the wall or fence. Don't go back to it only as a reminder and not as a steady thing. Our main objective at this point has been to make the horse understand that by getting back and having his hind legs well under him, he can make this move at a walk and it does not hurt him. Once he has found this out, we will start somewhat different tactics to further it. That's it for openers. Our next step will be to work this horse away from the wall. Proceed at a walk around the arena, but stay away from the fence or wall.

We are training this horse to pivot as it's called for participating in a reining contest. It is just the beginning of our teaching him to do a three hundred sixty-degree turn. In other words, a complete circle to right or left. When just the pivot was required, trainers made the mistake of getting the horse to do a short distance pivot to the left, then come back to center and do a short pivot to right. It's been my experience that a horse's training on these short pivots would soon lead him to start to cheat on one pivot or the other. In other words, instead of making each pivot equally, he would make a long one in one direction, then a short one in the other. He would soon start to think that as long as he moved off the ground twice, he was done and doing it all right. So our aim will be to go clear on around in a complete circle, one or two in one direction and one or two in the other direction. This will make the horse think he's going to have to complete a circle at least once. Then when called upon to do a pivot left and a pivot right, he is fooled to the extent that he never knows which you are going to do, a three hundred sixty-degree circle or a pivot left or right. This keeps the horse from trying to cheat on these turns and will keep him from getting sour on them. I thought this might be worthwhile mentioning before we actually get into the pivots and eventually the three hundred sixty-degree turns.

As you recall we worked this horse against a wall or fence to get him to set back and more or less forced this action to get him to get off the ground in front to make a faster turn. It was to let the horse know he could achieve it. He found it wasn't too hard. What we have to consider here is the fact that it was the wall that forced him back, so his weight was on his hindquarters, making it easier for him to get it done.

We will now have to keep in mind that we will be working in the open. That we are again going to have to get this horse getting back on his rear quarters to enable him to swing around easier with his front feet off the ground to make a pivot or a three hundred sixty-degree turn. When the horse is going into a roll back, at the split second he stops with his hind legs well under him, he can make this complete about-face and jump out. So it does not pose the same problem that it does when he's at a stand-still, unless we figure out a way to get him setting back with his weight on his rear quarters. The thing he has to know is the fact that his pivot hind leg has to be under him. The one thing that is and will set him up for this move is a good light reverse on the horse. This calls for an immediate back for one step in response to the reverse cue and the reins.

Now if this horse has accepted spurs and leg cues okay and if they have been used right, we will be using them in this particular part of his training more so than we have in the past. We will be taking care not to overuse them. If we have been working our reverse on this horse along in our training sessions, he probably won't need much work on it. If not we will have to polish him up some more before teaching him to pivot. This is going to be done at a walk without a martingale. You can have your choice of bits. I would use a swivel shanked snaffle with the fork at the end of the reins secured to the snaffle.

Let us outline the measures we will use to get the horse started on these pivots. We will start out and work our horse for awhile to get the edge off from him. Walk and lope him in both leads, but we don't want him tired. So fifteen minutes of riding should have him settled down and ready for this new set of actions we will get him to do. Ride around at a walk for awhile away from the fence or wall. Then stop your horse. Give him a cue to back, pushing our feet ahead three or four inches (with spurs on), then pull lightly on your reins with hands down. Now before slacking your rein and assuming you are going to pivot left, rein to the left. Put your left leg in your horse's side. At the same time reach up and bump his right shoulder with your right stirrup very lightly. If your horse comes around to the left, and you know he has cleared the ground with his front feet to make the move, relax your reins. Pet your horse and pause a few seconds. Ride around again for a minute or two and repeat.

Now supposing he did not do it on this first attempt. Make another attempt right after the first one failed without riding him out. If he failed again, don't pet him. Simply ride off, but don't scold him either. Remember, when after walking around awhile, when you stop your horse, back him up enough to get that weight off his front end. Then rein him sharp to the left using a lifting action on your reins. At the same time reach up and spur him a little on his right shoulder, while holding that left leg in his belly or just behind the cinch. Also remember that the first time he comes off the ground let him set and reward him. You should now have a general idea as to what you are doing and what you're trying to do with the horse. You might also carry a bat and use it sparingly on his neck just behind your rein. Between the stirrup and spur and maybe the bat, the horse will soon be making quarter circles right and left. Remember, it's going to take some time to get a smooth pivot and three hundred sixty-degree turn on your horse, but it can be worked in on the same session as the other things you're teaching in your reining.

A word of caution might be well to put in here at this time. In your attempts to school this horse in making these quarter turns, do not at any time reward this horse by petting him if he does not move his body right or left in the direction you want him to go. If he came up in front a little without turning, this is not what you want him to do. If he is rewarded at this time, he will think that is what he was expected to do by your rewarding him for it. You just might be starting to teach this horse to rear up in front. So for sure don't encourage it. The way to counteract this action on his part is while in position and reining him either left or right for a pivot, reach down with one hand and pull his head down and to the side you want him to pivot on. If he is sullen and refuses to bend, pop him with that bat or hang that spur on his neck. Once a horse has felt that spur, after that just the threat of raising that stirrup and spur will usually make him think twice before refusing to turn. Once the horse is starting to pivot a little, then rewarded, make another pivot in the same direction. Get to a full half circle making two pivots. Then quit for that time. Walk around some more and try again, until you are making full half turns in both directions. I would not work on this pivot or three hundred sixty-degree turns for over fifteen minutes at each session.

A good hand position for this particular part of the horse's training, if using the bat, is to have both reins in one hand with palm down. The reins will be crossed in the palm with the end of each rein on each side of the horse's neck. You will also find out that if you set your rein about three inches shorter on the way your horse is turning it will help. This will keep his nose into the turn and his head will be in position. Once you are pretty well along and making three hundred sixty-degree turns both ways you can even up your reins. Your reins, however, should still come out of the bottom of your hand and be splitting them between thumb and forefinger with your wrist flexed down.

I will mention something here that came to me that perhaps I missed in the previous chapters. Good riders and trainers have to isolate their arms and hands from their body. They should not be influenced by the body movements in handling the reins. This calls for a lot of balance and can be helped by the novice if he has two reins in one hand, by placing one hand on the fork of the saddle to keep his position on the horse, and letting his other hand controlling the horse remain fluid and free from movements of the body. We are talking training here, and also for juniors while learning how to ride. You can always let go of the saddle horn, but trying to balance on those reins will soon wreck a horse's mouth in a hurry.

Let's say we are getting some pretty fair three hundred sixty-degree turns out of the horse down the line a couple of weeks later. Now we can almost be sure that we can make a pivot once to the left and once to the right, because the horse is expecting to make a full three hundred sixty-degree turn. So once in awhile take him for a pivot left and one right. Then alternate a three hundred sixty-degree turn one way and a pivot or quarter turn the other. Then stop.

This whole thing on a reining horse is to out think him and make and keep him working without his being able to figure out a way to scotch or sour on you. But once you have a horse doing a thing don't overdo it. Do just the opposite. Put less time on it. But what time you do spend on it do it with the thought in mind of improving on it. A horse gets tired of being forced to do the same thing over and over again and under pressure. It's a good idea to just saddle him up once in awhile and just ride him. He will enjoy the change from the training routine and it will play an important part in reviving his interest the next day out. I believe it takes eight months to turn out a good reining horse. It's a slow, steady build-up and a gradual improvement on everything he does. There are no ninety-day wonders among the good trained reining horses.

Remember that this horse has got to have a good, light, straight back with mouth closed and nose tucked. There are several methods, but in all honesty, I got it done best with a rein in each hand at the beginning and those spurs would be used hard enough to get it done. Once I'd accomplished it, I could cue for a back by just pushing both stirrups ahead about four inches. The horse sees this forward movement and when put lightly into the bit with a little pressure on those reins wanted to back up and did. He might need a little tuning up as a reminder, but I would say he's a light backing horse for life.

On these pivots and three hundred sixty-degree turns on your final finish in training, you should be using the following cues. His first cue when at a stop would be to move both stirrups ahead about four inches. Then come back on both reins putting him into the bit and brought back about a foot onto his hindquarters. The second cue is the leg in his side. Then the neck rein is applied. This is the way he determines which way he's going to turn. When he feels the leg in him and maybe just the spur resting against him, he will put his left hind leg in position under him prior to the pivot or three hundred sixty-degree turns. When calling for just the pivot to the left, he sees your right foot up and ahead about two or three inches as a threat from that side. Once he completes a pivot left, you reverse your leg and rein positions to just the opposite to bring him back to the right.

In wrapping up this writing about pivots and three hundred sixty-degree turns, we might add here, once the horse is in the turn slack up on your reins a little bit while he's in the act. Take up again for the next one. This gives him a split second on each pivot so he can retain his balance. He also enjoys relief from the bit pressure.

Then we may talk a little about the reason for putting the leg and spur against his side. This is done for two different reasons. One is to let the horse know before the neck rein hits him, which way he's going to turn. This will prepare him for the coming rein. It's also used to hold that side and leg of the horse still while making the turn. You must not spur this horse on the side while holding your leg in him. If you do he will move his rear end away from the spur as he comes around in front, and he will be spinning by moving his front quarters. At a split second later, he will move both hindquarters away from your leg and spur. You don't want a spin but four pivots to make the full turn with your horse's one leg remaining primarily in the same spot. This is why we call it his pivot leg. If he spins and moves his hindquarters every time he moves his front quarters, he's actually not pivoting on the one leg, but spinning using both ends of his body.

 **18**

Roll Backs

In reining pattern number one a horse is required to do a roll back past a marker on each end of the reining pattern. A roll back over the hocks is accomplished by the horse when he is going at a fast lope. He then has to gather up and do a complete about-face and jump out in the opposite direction. At some point in this maneuver the horse should come to a complete stop with his pivot leg under him. At the split second that he stops, he wheels around on his pivot leg and uses that leg as a springboard to propel himself out of the turn and back into a fast lope. This requires the horse to be in the proper lead at the time he makes the turn. This is why we have taken the pains to put solid flying changes of leads on the horse prior to his roll back training. To get this job done right, the horse has to be able to respond to the rider's cue for a change of leads behind at any given point.

By way of explanation of the importance of the hind lead changes using the number one pattern as an example, the horse having made two figure eights in the pattern comes out of the last figure eight in his left hind lead traveling in a semi-circle. His next move will be to go past the marker and make a left roll back. As he heads for this marker, he should be changed to his right hind lead to make it possible to bend in a straight line by the marker. He will then gather up and change to a left hind lead using his left leg as a pivot to complete a left roll back. As he completes this roll back, he should come out in his right lead as he is using his left leg as a pivot leg. His right leg will move forward first putting him in a right hind lead. Then as he heads for the opposite end of the pattern to do the second roll back, to enable him to get it done smoothly he must be in his right lead. If by chance he came out of the first roll back in his left lead, in his scramble to jump out, he must be switched back to a right lead. Then as he gathers up he brings his right leg under him to make the right roll back and runs out for his final stop to be followed by the pivots. I have described this to show you how important the hind lead changes are. If the horse does not execute them properly at the exact point they should be used, he cannot and will not be able to make these difficult moves.

You will often see a reining horse make one perfect roll back past one marker, then do a sloppy one on the other end. The reason was that the horse was in position by being in the correct lead on the good roll back and in the wrong lead on the sloppy roll back. As the horse bends towards the spot where he is to make the roll back, and he does not make the hind lead change to permit him to get to that spot right, he will start to resist getting to the designated spot and will start to cheat on the spot that he is to make the roll back. Here again the hind lead change becomes essential. The rider should know on the second stride of the horse coming out of the roll back which hind lead the horse is in. In the horse's efforts coming out of the roll back, he could come out in either lead. Due to this fact, for the rider to make the second roll back correct, he must have control of the hind lead change to set the horse up for the second roll back. This can give you an idea of what a person riding a reining horse must know. It's essential, therefore, that if you are going to have a good solid, winning, reining horse, he has to have mastered those leads. This is why I've been a firm believer of the hind lead change first, as the horse should wait for a cue from the rider before changing leads.

I like to use some kind of markers at the spot where he's to do his roll backs to teach the young horse to roll back at the beginning of his training. Then after he's gotten the idea, I discontinue using them. I start at a walk and go from marker to marker. I'll go in behind one, and as we have already taught the horse to pivot and do a three hundred sixty-degree turn before these roll backs, it is fairly simple to go in behind the marker and put him in the bit. Apply a little pressure on our reins, put our left leg in him, and pivot him to a left about-face and walk out on the opposite side of the marker. I walk him down to the other marker and repeat it, only to the right. I'll do this about eight times that day. Then I will quit for that session. On the next session I'll repeat what I did the first time about three times at a walk doing the same thing by cuing the horse for a left pivot behind one marker, then right pivot on the other. Then I'll trot this horse in behind each one, but I'll try to get an about-face or a roll back from him instead of one pivot. I'll probably have to make two successive pivots to get it done. Up to this point we have done this slowly using the markers to teach the horse to identify where we expect him to come around. We acquaint him with the idea that he is expected to go in there, stop, get his weight back on his rear quarters and come around with his front end off the ground and come on out. When he's doing fairly well and starting to anticipate, at this point, that he is going to stop, then wheel. I'll change the tactics. I'll put him into a right lead. Put on a little speed at a gallop. Go in behind the marker and cue for a left lead. At the second I feel he has made the change, I'll cue for a stop by using his neck stop. Put my left leg in him, and put my right foot up and out just a little to threaten him, at the same time bringing my right neckrein across his neck. When he is facing out the opposite direction, I'll jump him out easy in a lope. Then after about fifty feet, I'll stop him, pet and reward him.

I'll walk the horse down about fifty feet from the other marker and put him in a left lead. Put on a little speed faster than a lope. Go in behind the marker. Call for a right change of leads. When I feel the change, I put my right leg and spur in his right side, put him in the bit, and put the left neck rein on him. I'll also raise my left stirrup towards his left shoulder and threaten him with the spur. I'll get what kind of a turn on his hindquarters that I can get, and jump out at a lope. Again I stop before going back to the other marker. I'll reward the horse and pet him. I won't discipline at this time for whatever he does that isn't right. He has not had enough practice to know in his mind whether he is doing right or wrong. He is going to have a lot of these repeated short runs on these roll backs to make progress right. We will never at this stage hook those figure eights and our roll backs together. You will be eager to try it but don't. It will end in a bad run and just get your horse shook up for nothing. You'll be disappointed.

The main reason I've stopped between each roll back is to give this horse a breather and let him tackle them while he's cool and level headed and can think. Once your horse is shook up and puffing, you might as well say it's a bad session. Walk him around to cool him out and don't get mad at him. If you know or suspect he's really trying, be satisfied. He will improve. So don't worry about it.

After about a week of using these markers to designate to the horse where he is going to make a roll back, he's ready to do both of them hooking the run together. I do this by starting further away from the first marker. Let's say about two-thirds of the way down from the other one. I'll start him at a gallop in his left lead. About fifteen or twenty feet from the marker, I'll change him to a right lead behind. This time I won't cue for a left turn but just bend him over my left leg as I pull upon my reins. By this time he knows he's going to make a left roll back. As I pull him to a stop with my leg in his side, I would expect him to position that back foot on his own when coming to the stop. He may have to take one more step to get it under him, but since he's already gathered going into the bit and reins, he should come out in his right lead, then head directly down to the other marker for a right roll back. Then when he rolls back, he does so on the right leg and foot. This is why it's so important that the horse has to have a good cued change of leads. He doesn't know any better and if he's not good on his leads, you are unable to help him. This is why there are not many good reining horses. People run these horses on these patterns and flounder through them. Part of the time the old pony knows what he is doing and part of the time he doesn't. Also part of the time the rider knows what the horse is doing and part of the time he doesn't know what he himself is doing. So you can well imagine what kind of a run the result is going to be. To make a good run on any of the many patterns they are running today, you really have to have a good schooled horse, or you might just as well have stayed at home.

Now we have got a change of leads on this horse. We have gotten him schooled on three hundred sixty-degree turns. This also improves his pivots. While we are schooling this horse, we have made sure that he will stop and stay quiet on a slack rein. If you have taken enough time and have broken these different actions down to individual acts and not crowded your training on patterns, this horse should do any of them. When finished with each one, he should be able to keep calm and remain that way.

I like this going from one roll back to the other using quite a bit of distance because it has a good effect on this horse not to anticipate a stop between them. He gets kind of like a barrel horse. They like to run and get into action pretty fast in their eagerness to get to the point where they are going to roll back. Here again you should not overdo it. Three or four of these sets of roll backs is enough to make sure that we don't come up with a charging horse.

While in the process of doing these changes of leads and roll backs, it's important that you ride the lead that the horse is in. Your shift of weight should come in the exact execution of the lead change. Do this lightly. Don't overdo it by throwing your weight too far either way. If overdone, you will cause your horse to get out of balance with your weight. He won't be able to get himself back under your weight properly. The shift of weight is done smoothly. You will be riding your horse with your weight pretty much in the middle of him and just a little more weight on the lead he's in. When calling for a change, shift your weight to the lead you are calling for. Raise up a little in your stirrups at the same time coming back with your reins to check your horse just a little. Then cue him with your off leg asking him to change behind. Once you feel the shift of his body behind, shift your weight to that lead. Release the rein pressure and let him go on. The smoother you can ride a reining horse the better he looks and the better you look. There is nothing more beautiful to watch than a free, flowing, reining horse going through these patterns. It takes some teamwork of man and horse to make it that way. Reining horses that can do it all are not too plentiful nor will they ever be.

Here again we might mention the weight in relation to the roll back. You can knock a horse out of position to make a smooth roll back if you are not with him. In other words, once he starts a roll back your weight should be on that side he's turning on. At the split second he comes out, you should be sitting ahead on him and off the rein. If you are setting back on him, and at the same time have not released him, you will cause him to come out high with mouth open and will look bad. You would not have helped your horse at all. I don't like to see a horse come into a roll back on a long slide and roll back. I think a horse is out of position with legs too far under him to make a roll back properly. I like him to come in and gather up. Then when his feet feel right for him to make it and with practice he'll figure that part out, he will gather up enough where he can execute this turn smooth and in balance. Some horses are versatile enough where they can get both roll backs equally as well. A lot of horses will make a terrific roll back one way and a sloppy roll back the other. So if it's repeated and noticed that one is much better than the other, you should go back to the one he's awkward at and do a lot of singles, making sure the horse is in the proper lead. Practice on the one roll back that he's failing on, until he's improving on it. By concentrating on a mistake, it can save you some bad moments down the road at a show. If a horse is working with a much too high-headed position on roll backs, put him back in a martingale. You may have to go back to a different bit also to smooth him out. A lot of horses have a tendency to work high-headed, and if not restrained and trained down, will work higher and higher.

You may need some help on some of these mistakes a reining horse makes. If you can't figure out what's causing him to make them, don't wait too long. There should be somebody in your area that has the knowledge about a certain move the horse is making wrong. Don't hesitate to ask for help. I'd not ruin the horse. I would seek the help, if it were there. Nobody knows it all. A lot of inexperienced people are guessing a lot of the time, but are too proud to ask for some sound advice. We are all proud, but let's not let it keep us from asking for advice. We might keep from spoiling a pretty good horse. I've seen novices do more with a horse than some trainers I've known. They were getting away with bluffing their way through for years, sometimes blaming a good horse because of their own lack of knowledge.

I've tried to cover these roll backs and to give the right kind of instructions on them in simple terms that you can understand. If you study what I've told you or refer back to them when you run into a problem and you take time to think a little, you might be asking yourself some questions. Each part of this horse's training has been done one thing at a time. This is giving a horse a chance to tuck into his memory each action apart from the others. He has also been taught that he's been given a prior signal or cue as to what he is going to do before he is asked to do it. By having used this method, we do not start on a new thing until the horse has pretty well in mind what he's been doing and is doing it fairly well. If he's failing in one thing, it should be concentrated on and worked upon before he is ready for a new subject. Most of them are related in the movements of the horse. If he lacks the knowledge to get one thing right, it will lead to his failure to accomplish some of the others.

Remember in reining, you have to be looking ahead to where you're going. What you're going to do and still be thinking of how you're riding your horse, cues, rein pressure, weight shifting, and riding the lead. When you get this all through your head, and the horse has gotten it through his head, you have covered a lot of ground.

Assuming we have a horse that is three or four years old and is not broke, or a horse that is broke but has not had much training done on him. I would say that this kind of a horse to be successful as a competition reining horse would have to have a lot of work done on him before we actually got into reining training with him. My methods of training this horse for reining would have included ninety percent of the training described in this book, prior to actual reining training for competition purposes. Then I would bet a lot of money he would be a success in anything I wanted to do with him, if he had had the right kind of basic training. The one thing I might have questioned would be, after I had finished him as a pleasure horse, whether or not he had the ability to make an all-around horse. I believe if given the time, and we are now talking about a year's training, that the good horse could compete in any of the events or all of them successfully. If he were also halter material, we would be looking towards a champion. It sure would be a pleasure to own such an animal. I've never been lucky enough to own one, but have worked such horses for other people.

 **19**

Stops

On the subject of stops, I'm going to point out the contrast between a reining horse stop and a rope horse stop. A rope horse stop is probably one of the most unique and the most coordinated actions a western horse does. I'm sure many of you have seen ropers go into a roping box, then giving the calf a head start, see the horse run up to a calf (after the roper has roped the calf) and put on a stop that started and completed in one stride with his rear legs under him. A split second later a roper has used this stop to propel him in the direction of the calf. He then ties the calf in eight to eleven seconds flat. There is probably no higher tribute to a horse's coordinated action as is the rope horse in his stop. I'm going to write a series of instructions on the rope horse later. I'm mentioning the rope horse stop here to demonstrate how coordinated a horse can get in this particular area.

We will now compare the rope horse stop in contrast to the reining horse stop. The roper does not want a long slide on his horse. If a horse would slide as long and as far as the reining horse's sliding stop, he would be hindering the roper instead of helping him. The roper wants his horse to get in the ground and stop that calf as quickly as he can. So the rope horse is taught from going from full speed to setting down by bringing his hind legs down and under him in one quick long stride. He does not move his front legs except to brace and break his rear action. Whereas on the reining horse it's not uncommon for the horse to come into a sliding stop with two even tracks made by his hind legs a length and one-half to two lengths of his body. The marked difference in stops is the fact that the horse in calf roping prepares himself for that two hundred or three hundred-pound jerk that follows his stop. He will brace his front legs in front for that weight and jerk to absorb the shock. Where the reining horse on a long slide does not have this weight facing him, will have to move one front leg once or more to complete a long slding stop. He does not brace his legs in front and as long as he makes a square sliding stop, he is not scored down by judges for moving his front legs.

Now let us take a look at the position the rope horse is in at the completion of his stop. His rear quarters are down under him in an extremely squatting position. His head will be up and will be in line with his body as he completes this stop. Seldom do you see the long sliding, reining horse's head up in this high a position. If he is stopping correctly for a long slide, his head will be up higher than he would normally carry it in a moving ahead position. The horse uses his head and neck for balance in stopping. If pulled too high or too hard on the reining horse, it will cause him to be out of balance and keep him from executing a long slide.

Now let us take a rope horse and the different signals he has to prepare for his hard short stop with hindquarters under him. Some ropers want a horse to stop only when they throw their slack. So the horse is watching the rope, and when he sees the rope pulled shut, then the loose part of the rope between the roper's hand and that of the calf thrown up, he knows the roper has made a catch. When he sees the slack in the rope thrown forward away from him towards the calf, this is one of the signals he has to stop. Another signal that he has to prepare him for a stop is as the roper gets ready to rope, he will get off the horse's loins in preparation to throw. He does this, not thinking of helping the horse to stop by lightening up the hindquarters, but to better see the calf and steady his body to make an accurate throw. The horses sees the loop leave the roper's hand and executes the stop. So here are two distinct cues that the rope horse uses to stop. Another signal he has is the shifting of the rider's weight when he dismounts. These cues are repeated constantly in the early days of the horse's training, making from five to ten stops per roping session, sometimes every day for weeks. This gives the horse an opportunity to develop this hard stop.

I've talked about the rope horse here to point out that a horse, if certain things are used in teaching the stop, can and does develop to a high degree in his ability to stop. One thing is certain, signals have to be given the horse prior to a stop other than snatching his mouth in hauling on the reins. So we will get back to the reining horse stop and how to go about getting him to do it.

We will work with this horse at a slow lope to teach him his first stops, and to get him to gather up prior to it, to get the slide effect. Some people like to use the same spot to get a stop started on a horse. However, I prefer to lope this horse around a little then as I've already described, the use of our neck stop throughout his training to save his mouth. We are going to enlarge on this part of it and explain why it is one of the easier ways to get it done. With a shanked snaffle bit on the horse, we will start off loping around the arena. We are going to be sitting down on this horse for this part of his schooling. We will also be riding him with our legs resting against his body but not hugging his belly. As we go on around, and when we come to a spot we have picked to stop, we will do the following things when coming to this stopping point: We will have a rein in each hand. Move both hands forward touching this horse just back of the crest on his neck. Don't leave your hands there but a split second. Then come back with a steady motion. Make contact with his mouth, don't jerk, but with a steady pull with your hands coming back just below your belt line. Now just prior to what you have done with your hands on the neck stop, raise your body up putting your weight forward. Turn your toes slightly out and squeeze your horse with both legs. While you are doing this and you know what lead the horse is in when coming into the stop, you will bear down on that stirrup on that lead. Then as the horse starts to set down bring your weight back so that it is evenly distributed on the horse. In the process of the stopping action of the horse, your hand pressure on your reins will be just enough to steady the horse and keep him straight. At the completion of the stop, release the squeeze on the horse with your legs. Straighten your feet. This will take the spurs away from your horse. Your last action will be to release the pressure on your reins.

In your first attempts to stop this horse you will not expect him to slide. Let the horse stand at the completion of the stop for perhaps a minute. Then back him up a few steps. Turn off center and go in another direction at a walk. If you do this every time you stop, you will be teaching your horse to believe he gets a breather at the end of each stop, lessening his chances of getting shook up in the early stages of his training. I will stress here that you put considerable distance and galloping time between stops. Use a different place to stop each time. Make sure the ground you are working on is not too dug up and loose. Also that it is not too hard and rough.

Good long sliding stops are accomplished by using cues prior to stopping and not repeated too often. As the horse acquires the knowledge of what's expected of him and he is improving, you will stop him less. You will also concentrate more on your posture and your cues and your rein pressure to get them done smoothly.

No matter what kind of a stop the horse makes in his first week's training, don't get discouraged. There is a lot more coming in teaching this horse a sliding stop.

His feet should be carefully looked at before we start this stopping training. As I've mentioned before, I'd rather use an old pair of shoes on the rear feet, ones that have been worn off on the toe, but are not thin on the sides. If you use a new set of shoes, you will dub or grind off the toes of the shoes. You should also make sure that on your front shoes there is not a fraction of an inch protruding at the heels. This might let the hind shoe hook the front one. You will also have skid boots on this horse in back. You might use ankle boots in front, as the horse could overreach in his training and nick himself to the point where you have to lay him up for a time.

Now let's get back to the stops. Each time you stop this horse, once he is stopped, back him up a little and let him set for five or six seconds or longer if you like. Then turn him off away from the line of travel and walk out. Then start into a lope again and pick out a different spot ahead of you where you are going to stop. Don't be afraid to put quite a bit of distance between stops. The ground you are working on here is important. Do all your work from now on with those skid boots on. You will have worn out a pair of skid boots by the time you have gotten a good stop on this horse. For sure don't try to stop hard without them. Once a horse has his heels burned a few times, he will quite trying to get into the ground. Make sure you adjust them right, so they are not too tight on the adjusting straps. If it calls for a new hole to make them fit, get your leather punch and use it. Keep the horse's feet as comfortable as possible. Clean his feet before you use him. Don't spare the farrier, but watch him. They are sometimes in too big of a hurry. Tell him not to take off to much sole or he is liable to make him tender and sore him up.

Let's go over this procedure once again. As your horse gets stop on his mind, and this will be after about six sessions, every time you stop this horse, don't use any more pressure on those reins than you have to. Don't depend on your reins to stop your horse. Do not haul him. This means running out there and slamming that bit on him. In other words, don't grab him with your reins. The reins should be handled in this manner. Take out the slack first. Then when you are in contact with his mouth ease it on him. Increase it using it like you would a wheel brake on your car. Pull lightly on him at first. Remember, he has two signals at this time that you are going to stop. The first one, the neck cue, is definite and he for sure knows what it is for. The locking up of your legs on his body plus your shifting your weight up and onto the lead prior to stopping him are two more, plus putting him lightly into that bit as your hands come away from the neck stop. He has plenty of time to get these signals. Don't grab his neck. Just use both hands and touch it lightly and come down and back. By the time you are taking up on your reins he will already be in the act of gathering up to stop.

Use your martingale about the second week if necessary. Then go to two reins in one hand. Use that rein hand to touch his neck and use the other hand on the fork of your saddle to help position and practice your body moves. Forget about how you look, and train your horse. I might even mention here, from time to time, you will have people watching you. Don't let them affect you to doing things with your horse you would not do if they weren't there. This is a natural thing. We all like to look good and show off a little. Fight it and never, never put a horse on something new that he has not done or been trained to do, to demonstrate what a good horse you have got. You will wind up loser if you do.

When out of the martingale, you can start changing one tactic. We have used a martingale and a rein in each hand enough to get the horse to stop square and to let him know he can do it without looking at the sky. As he learns to gather up and slide a little you can go on with him without the martingale or go back to it if necessary, if you handle your reins right. Keep your rein hand as low as possible. Use your palm down with your reins coming out of the bottom of your hand split between your thumb and your forefinger. You also must keep your rein arm and wrist flexed. You should make sure your reins are even. Even one-half inch difference is too much. Don't be afraid in training to use that free arm to help you position your body. It will also help you in your efforts to isolate your rein arm from your body. Remember, we are training a horse. Any and all things we can do to help him we should do. Looks come later. When you have a horse that works well and looks good, you will look good. But no matter how hard you try, if the horse doesn't look good in his actions, you won't either. I'll add here, I don't think a horse should be stopped hard over five or six times per session once he is improving on his stopping. Too much hard stopping will sour him on stops in a hurry.

After the first attempts to get this horse to slide and even at his first success in a small way in making a slide, reward him each time he does it by voice and patting him. This will encourage and induce the horse to continue in his efforts. It will help him to understand that the slide is what we are trying to accomplish. After a horse is stopping fairly well, at some point you will have to make the transition from neck stop to a drop or shake of your reins before putting him in the bit and before you pull on those reins. Here is how it is done. You should do this by keeping the proper rein position. This position should never be where your rein hand has to move over an inch to an inch and one-half to make contact with your bit. Then your hand when coming back should travel just a short distance. This will put your hand in the proper position contacting your horse's mouth. The hand should be palm down and reins coming out of the front of your hand with wrist flexed down.

Now I'll describe to you what the horse notices on this neck stop, after it has been repeatedly applied. When you move your hand with the reins in it to touch the horse's neck, he sees and feels the slack come down in the reins. From this he knows the next instant your hand is going to touch his neck. Start to use the same amount of slack but don't touch his neck. Once more, flick your hand in a quick downward fashion so the slack is obvious to the horse. Then take out the slack slowly and put him in the bit. It's a matter of timing. Give him that quick drop of your rein hand. Then come back and up until he stops. Pause there on a loose rein. Then go on. He soon will get to stopping with a quick drop in the slack in the reins instead of the touch on the neck.

Now you have been stopping this horse on loose ground in an inside or outside arena. Your horse is starting to get in and slide. But let us say that you have been using the fence or wall to help the horse to stop straight. Now change the pattern a little. Proceed around the arena and know what lead your horse is in. Then stay in that lead, but come down the center. Pick up a little speed, faster than a lope. When you start down the middle, put your horse in the bit just enough where he can feel it but no pressure. Look up ahead to the place you're going to stop. Then put your free hand on the fork of the saddle to support your body. Flick your reins in the way we just described, and come back on your reins. Just before the rein shake, raise up in your saddle pushing down on the stirrup on the lead side. At the same time squeeze your horse. Now instead of hauling the mouth of your horse, just pull hard enough to steady the horse. If you pull too hard, you will bring him up in front. His head will come too high and his mouth will gape open. If you try to put a good stop on your horse strictly with your rein pull, you will wind up having to pull harder all the time. So pulling on the reins is not the answer.

If you keep running out as you would on a reining pattern run and keep stopping in the same area, it won't be long before your horse will get reluctant to run out free. Then when he gets to where he's been stopping, he will start to anticipate the stop. He will start to show signs of scotching or setting up before you cue him. So you have to have room. Don't stop in the same place all the time Do not overstop him. That is making too many stops in one training session. If you are going to stop a lot in the center of the arena, or when you are practicing a pattern, which you will do once in a great while for a test on the horse. Do quite a few individual roll backs not hooked to the pattern. After doing a couple of roll backs at a pretty good speed, pick a spot and throw a stop on this horse. Alternate the roll backs. Do a series of two or three and don't stop hard. Then do two or three and put a stop on the horse. The next day stop at a pretty good speed along the wall. But remember, don't fool the horse on your rein position. Prior to going into that stop, raise your rein hand a little higher and connect lightly wih his bit. Then give the reins a quick drop or shake. Wait a split second, then a steady light pull back, riding the right body position and weight on the lead he's in. As you apply the squeeze on this horse, both spurs should be resting against the horse's side where he can feel them, but you will actually not be spurring the horse. At the split second the stop is completed, get your spurs away from the horse's sides. The good sliding stop demands coordination between rider and horse. The horse has to have prior cues that he is going to stop and the timing and execution of the cues by the rider is important here. It will take time and patience to put it all together.

 **20**

Rope Horse Phase I

To become a roper is a long road to start down for any one. It can lead to quite a bit of expense. So before an individual makes up his mind that he's going to go through with learning the art, he wants to consider what it's going to cost. The amount of time involved to learn, and the cost of stock, meaning calves or steers, also whether or not there are others in the area interested in the same project. There are a lot of roping clubs in most parts of the country. There's a good chance there is somebody among them who would be capable of giving others instructions. These men or most of them do not have enough horse savvy to produce or train a good rope horse. This calls for a lot on a trainer's part, and he will have to have started and trained from twenty to thirty head of different calf horses before he can have become any kind of an authority on the subject. The trainer should also be a fair roper. Good calf roping horses are hard to come by. They are a good deal like reining horses that are consistent. They come in all sizes and colors. One thing he has to have bred into him is speed. A horse can start and run so fast. If after he's doing everything a calf horse should do and excelling at it, if he can't catch up with a calf and gets outrun, all of his training is lost as far as a money winning competition horse is concerned. You can teach a horse most anything if you have the knowledge, but you can't give him more speed if he doesn't have it.

Calf horses break down into about three categories. There's an old campaigner that has a lot of age on him and changes hands every so often. As a roper gets better through practice, he goes out and gets a better and faster horse hoping he can win on him. This first horse is what we would call a practice horse. This horse usually lacks speed. He's been hauled to rodeos by amateurs and won on a little, but is discarded for some of the following reasons: He has no speed. He doesn't stop good. He doesn't score good.

He's box simple. He won't work a good rope. He won't rate a calf. He's rank and can't be trusted. He doesn't haul good. These are most of the things calf horses are counted down for.

Then there's a mediocre rope horse. He has speed. He is a good box horse, but won't rate a calf. He runs one too close or won't stop consistent. Every once in awhile he will make a flawless run and the roper wins a go-round on him. The second go, he will do something just a little different. He fails to help a roper enough or overworking a rope too much. Anyway just enough to keep him in the middle class. Now money can buy these first two types without you going in hock. The first type sells for anywhere from six hundred, seven hundred, or nine hundred and fifty dollars. The middle class goes up from a thousand to two thousand dollars. The last class, the third and top horses, from twenty-five hundred dollars to you name the price. The buyers for the first class are ropers just starting out to rope. They use them until they think they can beat an Oliver or Ferguson. Then they buy the second type horse and hit the road. When they grow tired and are convinced that they can't hit or make the top fifteen in the nation, they start roping for fun and a little money. This class of ropers would want a pretty good price for this kind of horse and would probably get it because they have a lot of fun and entertainment with him.

The big figure horses don't change hands too much and if they do it's because he's got one little flaw in him. It won't be noticed by average calf ropers even if they owned him. These are the calf horses that will be at the bigger purse rodeos throughout the country. So much for rhetoric about rope horses. I think it is time to go to schooling a rope horse. I have been successful on most horses I've trained.

I'll not get into arenas or calf chutes. I will, however, say that the arena in or outside must be big enough if you are going to go all the way in training a calf roping horse. The arena should V up at the roping box and chute, and should be at least two hundred feet long and sixty feet wide with a holding pen at the center on the opposite end of the arena opposite the chute end. The end of this arena should be rounded off so when schooling your horse and in tracking or following a calf, he won't be hanging up in the corners. The receiving pen should also be to the outside of the rounded arena and in the center. When the receiving pen gate is closed, the end of the rounded arena should be one rounded curve. So a calf won't hesitate at any obstruction there.

One word about young ropers. Don't learn to ride on a rope horse roping calves. Get some old horse and ride, ride, and ride. You should be a pretty good rider before getting on a rope horse and starting to rope. Another bit of advice is learn to handle a rope and learn to rope on the ground on a dummy sawhorse-type calf. A bale of straw or hay also makes a good target. You should also learn to handle and tie calves on the ground before you start roping. You will have wound up a hundred miles of rope and thrown thousands of loops before you have reached the stage to mount a horse and start roping. What extent or lengths you go in the above instruction is up to you, but if you do it, you will save yourself a lot of heartaches, caused yourself to be involved in less wrecks and will be able to refrain from spoiling a rope horse. Also you won't have to blame the horse for all the mistakes that you will be going to make. To be a good roper you have got to like to rope. It's a kind of fever. I suppose other athletes in other sports experience the same feeling. If you are not really dedicated to roping, I would suggest that you don't start. You can't like it today and hate it tomorrow. You have got to like to rope, win, lose, or draw to make it.

Now let us say that this horse we have been reining has some speed bred in him and has proven that he can change leads behind. He can do a roll back and has a good mouth. This horse as a four-year-old looks like and should be a good rope horse prospect. He's also got a stop on him. Sounds like he is almost made to order, doesn't he? We don't know how he's going to react to the handling of a rope on him. Let's say if he's gentle, we won't do anything with the horse the first week but carry a rope on him. We will drag it on both sides of him. Turn him into it so that he gets the feel of it around his rear quarters both ways. We will not have this rope tied hard and fast to the horn, but be carrying it in one hand or the other. When he doesn't mind this rope being around or touching his body, just set on him. When he's standing still, throw this rope out with a loop in it on both sides of his head. Stand up in your stirrups and throw over his ears. Don't touch his ears with it. We mean throwing the rope straight out over his head. Keep this up. Coil up and keep throwing in all directions from this horse, until he is not paying any attention to it. Then have an object that you can rope that is loose in the arena. It shouldn't weigh over forty pounds. One that can be roped easy and a rope won't slip off. An old stump or thirty-gallon drum makes a good object. Now go up to this object at a walk. Rope it and back your horse up. Take a wrap around your horn and tighten. He'll be surprised when the object moves as the rope tightens. He will soon get over it. Then turn the other way and with the wrap still around your horn pull this object around. Its bumping action and noise will scare him at first, but keep at it until he's not paying any attention to it. Drag it on both sides of the horse. I would not wind him up in the rope while tied to the object even with just a rap on the horn. He could still get tangled up in it with the weight on the end. Do this until this horse is absolutely used to this rope. On the more broncy-type horse, I put them in a small pen. I hobble him in front and just keep dabbing loops on him until he is standing quietly in the hobbles. I'd rope him around the neck a lot of times. I rope the cantle on the saddle, letting the lower end of the loop drop behind and around his hocks. Then slowly draw it up until he

Chain device to get a horse to work a rope

Photography by Neil Mishler, Ponca, Nebraska

was used to it and wasn't fighting the hobbles. At all times on this horse or on the ground make sure you don't hurt him with the rope. We are trying to teach him that the rope will not hurt him. We just want to get him used to the feel of it, and lose any fear of it when we are on him. The fear of a rope on the green rope horse will be enough that he won't pay attention as he should to the calves once we start him on them. If we do not use the above precautions, we might wind up with a horse that way.

We will now get into the dry run work on this horse and rope. Assuming he's gotten over his fear of the rope, I'll tell you how to make a piece of equipment that will work to get this horse to work a rope for the first time. Some trainers use just a neck rope for their first work in this part of the horse's training. I'm against it because you can't make a horse back straight up with it. They get the horse to work a rope, but it's usually with the horse backing in a semicircle. Once the habit is developed it is hard to correct. So I go to this other piece of equipment that will make the horse work a rope more carefully. In throwing slack at the horse with just a neck rope, you have to give him too much leverage.

To put this rig together go to your hardware to the chain department and buy fifteen links of flat, light oblong, link chain. These links can be from one inch to two inches long. Then purchase two rings that are two inches in diameter. This is all you need to buy here. Use a one-half-inch piece of latigo leather to make a headstall for your horse. Now take a hammer and flatten one ring so that it slips through the other. When this is done, tie each ring to each end of the chain using lace leather with several wraps. Count five links from the end of a ring and secure one side of your headstall to that link. Bring the headstall over the horse's head and bring the long length of chain across his nose and secure it to a link on the other end of your headstall. Before securing it to the headstall adjust the chain across the horse's nose to where it is just on the bridge of his nose. Reach under his jaw and bring the solid round ring that you have not flattened across under the jaw and slip the oblong ring through it. This is the ring that the rope will go through. When this chain tightens up the chain part connected to the oblong ring should be eight inches from the side of the horse's head. This will allow the horse to protect his jaw and have his head in the clear and to one side when the catch is made. If this equipment is adjusted right both rings will be on the right side of the horse's jaw. I would also emphasize that this chain will at all times remain loose around the horse's nose except after the rope is thrown with a calf in a loop, or when you are teaching the horse to work a rope while schooling him on the ground. If you are a left-handed roper you would, of course, have rigged this piece of equipment on the left side. I will add here that this equipment will be placed over all other equipment meaning bridle headstall, and tie down and will be at least two inches above the shanks on the bit.

We now have a piece of equipment that can get a horse to work a rope quicker and can control him while doing it with very little action on our part. It has to be used right, of course, to make it work. If you have been swinging a loop around and over his head, and he is not paying any attention to it, you can now run the end of your rope through this oblong ring on the chain and attach the horn loop of your rope to your saddle horn. Coil the rest of your rope up and hang it on the saddle horn also. Now mount your horse. Make sure there is enough slack in your rope between your chain and horn that it is not pulling on the ring on the chain. This also applies to enough slack between your hand holding the coil and the chain. Walk your horse around with one coil of your rope and your reins in your left hand and a loop in the other. Walk your horse straight down the center of the arena. Then pick an imaginary target out in front of you. Throw your loop out straight ahead of you. Take your left hand and put it on about the middle of his neck to stop him. Get down naturally with the horse standing straight. Then go down about ten feet in front of your horse. Reach down and pick up your rope and tighten it up. His first indication of what he will think you want him to do will be to come towards you as though being led. Slap him a little with that chain until he backs two or three steps. Then keeping the rope tight, let it slide through your hands and go down to the end of your rope. Holding out the slack, coil it up hand over hand. But don't slap this horse with it while you are going to him. Hang your coils on the right side. Pet your horse. Go around and mount up again. Sit on him a few seconds before picking up your reins and pat him some more. You sure should have a roping rein on your headgear. You don't want any dangling reins hanging down on this horse.

Now a little bit of psychology on what we are trying to get done on these dry runs. We are trying to get this horse to understand as long as this rope is tight nothing hurts him. But each time the rope wiggles or becomes slack, he gets hurt, unless he backs up enough to tighten this rope up. The reason we do not go clear to the end of the rope at the beginning is to teach this horse that right after we get down and this rope is picked up from the ground, he's supposed to start back. We will keep working this part of our schooling on this horse until we notice he is starting back on his own before we get to the ten-foot distance in front of him. But remember, do these things at first slow and deliberate. Give the horse time to figure it out and keep his cool. The first session just so he backs up every time you let the rope slacken, and he is making an attempt to take out the slack is good enough. Don't overdo it. Strive for a little improvement each day. Make sure you coil up your rope and go to him slowly, keeping the slack out. Hang your rope on the saddle horn and reward your horse. Remember from the first time you do this, you don't quit until he has backed up on that rope a little. Increase the distance each day. Then start to trot your horse. Swing a loop for ten or fifteen swings at a trot. Then throw it straight out ahead of him. Put a hand on his neck. Pull a little on the reins and get down straight with the horse. Repeat this a few times. Then do it at a lope. After about a week's sessions in this manner, and your horse is getting back as you walk towards the end of the rope, pick it up farther towards the end. Then holding the slack and watching the horse, start in a circle around him. Slap the chain at him making him get on back while you are circling him. He must hold a tight rope at all times. What you will be doing on the end of that rope is imitating what the calf movements will be later when he's actually chasing calves. While holding the rope tight, run two or three steps towards the horse letting some slack come in the rope. Then snap that chain and make him take it out. Once in awhile walk towards him and then wiggle the rope. Then snap him again until the rope is tight. Now you can overdo this also. You can overdo it to the extent that he gets scared of a rope. The horse has got to know that the split second you step down he starts back. So step down once in awhile and grab that rope about a yard in front of him. Force him to get on back but hold him straight so he goes straight back. Then let the rope slide through your hands until he has come to the end of it. Then at a down position with the end of the rope close to the ground, holler "whoa" at him. This will come in handy to help stop him when he overworks a rope with a calf on the other end later on.

Rope Horse Phase II

We have covered getting a horse to work a rope using a chain and a lightweight headstall to help us accomplish this important part of his schooling. By the way, any bit with shanks that is used in roping should have a bar attached to the bottom of the shanks so that when a rope is thrown it won't get caught on either shank of the bit. Tie downs are used on all rope horses. You should be using a light quarter-inch headstall with a nose band that fits around the animal's muzzle and set about where your bosal on a hackamore would set. It can be bought at most saddle shops or where western equipment is carried. There is the pencil-sized bosal with a small ring attached to the bottom. They are all right. Then there is a little flexible cable that is covered on the outside with a synthetic material. It is smaller than the others, but it will work and it is not as bulky as the pencil-sized type. The nose band on this tie down should be loose on the horse's nose. You have to adjust your bridle when you use them so that the horse does not sore up. The tie down strap is a little better than a yard long with a ring on one end. It is double on the end attached to your cinch for adjusting. There should be a snap attached to your cinch and a ring on the adjusting end of your tie down strap.

You should also have a breast collar on your horse. I like the type that has the strap coming over the neck of the horse just in front of the saddle. There are other kinds that just tie to each side of your saddle. Most late-model saddles have two little D-rings, one on each side of the saddle at the front of each skirt to buckle it to. I like to put my adjusting straps on my roping collar through my billet strap on the right side of the saddle and put the other strap between the wraps of my latigo so that the pull is more direct on the breast collar. Most roping collars have a ring in the center of them. Take a piece of lacing leather and make a loop about three inches long. Attach it to the ring in the center of the breast collar using it as a guide for the tie down strap. This makes more of a direct line from the cinch to tie down nose band on the head of the horse. The breast collar also serves as a place to carry the second loop. You won't use a second loop when practicing, but only when you have missed your first throw at a calf in competition. However, when the horse is fairly well along in his training, it would be wise to intentionally miss the first loop and let that rope drag while pulling the second loop and keep on running the calf to get the horse acquainted with the procedure, before you start to jackpot or rodeo for the first time. You won't be interested in it when first schooling your horse, because you will have all you can handle using one rope and not fouling it up.

A word here about stirrups in regard to roping. Most roping saddles come from the manufacturers with what is called a roping stirrup on them. However, there are several varieties on the market. There is one kind that I have had a preference for. It is known as the deep roper's stirrup and they are leather bound. This stirrup is deeper than the others. It weighs more due to the size. It has a tendency to stay in place better because of the weight. It is easier to get a boot into and out of faster than the lighter type. This lessens the drag on the right side when dismounting fast. It also gets your left foot out easier when leaving the horse. I would advise using the deep roper's stirrup in roping. I like them to train any and all stock horses also. Any hindrance by equipment that can be changed should be. When you total everything up in the selection of equipment, if it is the right choice, it can and does make a huge difference in the outcome of training horses. Equipment does not in most cases have to be the highest in price as long as it is the right kind for the job.

Another point to keep in mind is stirrup length while roping calves. You would ride a shorter stirrup length in roping than you would in ordinary balance riding. By riding a shorter stirrup length, it will enable you to get better observation of your target than a longer length. It will also enable you to be in a better position to get up and ahead on your horse when leaving the box. One full hole up might be too much using the holes that come in stirrup leathers. You might have to split the distance, using another set of holes that you would make yourself to get the correct position.

Now let us concentrate on calves and what would be the best kind to start this new horse on. Brahma calves are the standard roping calves used mostly throughout the country. But in the earlier stages of the young horse's roping training, to me, they have not worked out too well. Neither do we want calves that weigh over two hundred pounds. The slower the calves and the less fight they have, the better for this young horse. You would do real well to go out and buy five Holstein calves. Say calves about one hundred fifty to two hundred pounds that are on the doggie side and not wild. They will be best suited for your horse's first experience on cattle.

Turn these calves loose in the arena. Mount your horse and trail them around awhile. Don't run them. Just kind of get in behind them and follow them around in the arena. Let the horse smell them and watch them. Don't rope one. You might swing a loop and carry a rope with you. Watch his reactions to both cattle and rope while you are doing it. The next day pen your calves and turn one out. Leave the rest in the holding pen behind the chute. Close the gate and put a panel across the front of your roping box. You would also have your receiving pen at the opposite end of the arena closed. Now on this occasion you won't carry a rope. What you will be attempting to do is to get this horse to follow and rate a calf. You may have to go back to a ring snaffle and use a rein in each hand to get it done right.

You should run this calf around this arena and visualize in what position you want this calf in to rope him. The calf for a good shot should be almost straight in line with your horse. The calf should never be roped when he is more than a foot to the right of your horse's head. Later on when you've roped a lot of calves you will even want them just a little to the left of your horse. The reason the calf's position is important to you is that if he is too far to the right of the horse, you get what we call eyebrow catches or whisker catches. In this action the loop sets over the brow of the calf and does not come down on over the calf's nose so that you have him in the loop solid. That is one reason. The other reason is that if you do get him roped, when your horse stops the calf will not be jerked down, but is jerked sideways. He is also out of position when you go to the calf to tie him. The desired bust on a calf is that he come over backwards when hitting the end of the rope. This gives the roper a second's advantage to get to him just as he's getting up. It also seemed to me that calves busted in this way seemed a little more dazed and confused, adding to the roper's advantage to get him tied before he could react to kick out making him harder to tie. Thus throwing somebody out of the money if he did kick while being tied.

I have gotten off our first subject of rating calves on our green rope horse, but they are all related in the making of him.

Let's go back to tracking or rating the calf. We should begin this exercise by getting the horse in behind the calf. Don't crowd the calf. Just stay in behind him. At this point don't try to position your horse too much. This measure is to get the horse acquainted with the calf and his smell of him. When the calf turns, he turns always in behind the calf. As you repeat this procedure for three or four days, you will keep in mind the following: Am I too close to the calf? Is my horse covering the calf to the extent I can't get a shot at his head?

As this horse starts to get through his head that he's supposed to follow the calf, he will start to show some eagerness to do it. Most horses like to run after a calf and get a kick out of it. Then what follows is they want to get in too close to him once they catch up to him. I can't think of a worse habit to break a horse from than this one. So teach him early not to get too close. He should remain at least the length and one-half of the calf behind him. The horse in his eagerness to get at this calf will sometimes develop the habit of wanting to strike or bite the calf. Do not let your horse develop this habit as it, too, is very hard to correct. While teaching the horse to rate and track the calf, take it easy. Try to do one thing. Stay behind him and follow him putting the calf in position for the catch. Don't run one calf too long. Don't keep your horse going until he is out of wind and getting tired. It might be wise when tracking a calf to use your neck stop while going at a good clip and come to a complete stop. This will come in handy later when you start roping with a breakaway honda on your loop. After a week's tracking and following these bending calves without using the chute or box, and probably working your horse on them for from thirty minutes to an hour a day, you are ready to start breakaway roping, with just one calf in the arena and not using the chute or roping box.

In our former writing about working a rope, we will have taught this horse that every time this loop leaves our hand we have stopped this horse and gotten down. We have been taking pains to stop him straight and also getting down straight facing the calf. Then going down and picking up the rope, getting the horse to get back on the rope each time we got down. We will apply this in about the same way when we start to rope with a breakaway loop in actually hanging a loop around the calf's neck.

You can teach a horse a lot with a breakaway honda on the end of a rope. It has a whole series of advantages. You can teach the horse to follow and track calves. You can also get practice in roping for yourself prior to actually catching them in a solid loop. You can teach the horse to stop. You should get down each time whether you miss a calf or catch one. You can get him in the habit of getting back on the rope. It's easy on calves and serves a definite purpose all to your advantage. It gets you acquainted with where to rope a calf and where not to rope one. It lessens the chances of your getting hurt or your horse fouling up on account of the experience and knowledge that neither of you possess when you first start out.

Now let us say that you have gotten the horse following a calf that is alone in the arena. This time you put on skid boots behind and ankle boots in front. The front ones are optional, but the back ones are a must. You will also have the chain and headstall on the outside of your tiedown and bit. Now that you are going to be having both reins in one hand and are actually going to put or try to put this loop around the calf's neck for the first time, run the horn loop end of the rope through your ring on the chain. Make sure you have plenty of slack from chain to horn and slack from coil to chain. After getting on your horse and building a loop make sure that you have enough room between your loop and your coil of rope in your rein hand. Measure this distance by extending both arms each in the opposite direction. A full arm's length between coil and loop is about right. Maybe you can get by with a shorter distance but don't shave it too much between your loop and the coil of rope in your hand. It will cause your loop to fall short of the target if you do. Now double up your roping rein at the end and hold this rein with your little finger and the next finger to it. This puts your reins at the bottom of your hand. The one coil will be held with your top two fingers and your thumb. This will enable you to pull this coil lightly out of this hand after you have thrown your loop and are pulling in your slack.

You are now ready to start to breakaway rope this calf with the breakaway honda at the end of the rope. The type of breakaway to buy is cheap, in the neighborhood of a couple of dollars. If you can't buy one of them locally, they have them at most western supply houses. Maybe someone you know has one or two you can borrow. To get them to fit on a made-up calf rope, you have to remove the burner on your rope. Instead of buying new ropes that cost you from nine dollars and fifty cents to ten dollars and fifty cents apiece, seek out a roper friend and buy one or two from him that he no longer uses. Almost every roper has a couple he will part with for one-half price. He also might sell you a raggy piggin string. This is used to tie a calf's three legs after you rope him. These breakaway hondas we are talking about are made out of spring steel. They are about two and one-half inches long and resemble a slingshot crutch with an oblong loop at one end and a Y shape on the two ends. They are curled back in such a way they cannot injure a calf's eyes. To put them together you insert your honda on your rope between the loop of the U in the breakaway. Then the end of the honda slips over the Y end of the breakaway.

Roper and hand position applying neck cue stop

Photography by Neil Mishler, Ponca, Nebraska

179

Then pull it through your honda on the rope in the opposite direction until the Y of the breakaway is freely exposed. Now instead of running your rope through the honda, you simply push your rope into this spring steel Y and make your loop. These breakaways work okay. They will unbalance a rope somewhat and release a little too soon. So if you look close at the two little eyes on the end of the breakaway you will find them forming a small E on each end and they are curled back. Take a small piece of light cord or wrapping string that breaks easy when you test it with both hands in trying to break it. Then run it through these two little eyes once and tie it. This will cause your loop to stay on the calf longer, giving you a chance to learn how to handle slack. It will also give you time to throw and pull your slack and toss it away from your horse. At the same time put your left hand on your horse's neck on the crest. Pull lightly on your reins with your left hand. Then stay with your horse until he stops before you get down. Many horses are spoiled because riders bail off before a stop on the horse is completed. The roper going to the calf doesn't watch this horse close enough in the early stages of his training.

Now check out the following: Is your saddle okay? Have you got that breast collar right? Do you have a loop in the center to guide your tiedown? I think I forgot to tell you how to adjust this tiedown. Standing beside your horse on the left side with your tiedown connected, raise up on the jaw of your horse. You should be able to raise his head about eight inches above his withers before he hits the nose band on the tiedown. Do not put it lower, because it will interfere with your horse's ability to turn on a sharp bending calf. It will also hinder his stop. So now let us mount up and we will have one calf loose in the arena with all gates closed and no obstruction in our way. With rope and loop ready and as you approach the calf, bring your loop straight up. As you do this make the next turn of your loop over and above your head with the end of the loop clearing your horse's ears by about a foot. The end of the loop should be tilted down slightly to the front as it clears the head of the horse. Here is where all the groundwork you did on the dummy calves and hay or straw bales comes in handy. If you have done a lot of it, outside of clearing the horse's head, each time you swing your loop you should be able to keep the loop opening up on each revolution you make with your wrist. Run in behind that calf. When you think everything is about right and the calf is straight ahead of your horse and not too close, make one little extra harder turn with your loop. Throw and push down on this loop at the same time. Whether you miss or not, stop your horse. Go down and get the rope in about the middle and start the old pony back. Coil it up while going to him. Hang it on the horn and reward him.

Continue to use the slowest calf in the bunch for the first few days. Remember, position your horse on the calf. Don't take shots at the calf when he is too far left or right or too close to your horse. What you are trying to teach this horse is that you want to throw but will not throw until the horse is in the right position. He then gets to stop when you throw. He gets a little breather every time. You should keep this horse cool in these first sessions. He will school faster, stay settled more, and overall work better. If he gets hot and is puffing, quit. You won't make any more progress that session. Remember, roping and teaching your horse and yourself is going to take a lot of time.

When you have roped individual calves for about a week in the arena, it is now time to start thinking about using this horse in the box. If you have a friend that will load the chute and spring the latch turning out calves, use him. If you are lucky, you might find another roper to work with you for the privilege of roping a few of your calves after you have finished schooling your horse. Or your wife might be a good enough hand to do it for you. In any event you will have to have help from here on out.

 **22**

Rope Horse Phase III

We have started the horse on calves that are loose in the arena. We have been using a breakaway honda with the chain loose around the horse's muzzle. Our rope is running through the oblong ring on the chain. We will use the chain for a period of time in the box and until such time we are roping calves without the breakaway honda. It will have served a purpose. It has helped us teach this horse to back up straight. It has taught him to work a faster rope and has given us an advantage to teach him to stop.

We have started roping these calves with a breakaway honda on the end of our rope. We will continue to use it for some time. The breakaway being tied with a thin cord to give the calf a little harder jerk when he hits the end of the rope to break the string. It has also given this chain a jerk. It will teach this horse that if he is directly in line with the calf when the calf hits the end, he doesn't get hurt. If he is too far to one side or the other, the chain does hurt him. He will soon start to line up with the calves to avoid it. It also has another effect on the horse. He knows the chain is going to snap shut on his nose. If his head and that ring are in a direct line from the horn to the calf, it does not hurt him. So he does something else that is to the roper's advantage. He gathers up to stop, to beat that calf getting to the end of the rope to snap the chain. He also learns to get into the ground faster to avoid the snap on the chain. It is okay to be used in the box running calves with a breakaway, but I would not attempt to use it if I was inexperienced when roping calves solid and going down and tying them. If you happened to get the slack on the wrong side of the horse's neck, it could hurt him more than we would care to.

We still haven't roped a calf solid. So let's take off the break-away or exchange ropes. Instead of the chain, go to a neck rope. You can buy neck ropes in most saddle shops. Now you run your horn loop through the neck rope. Adjust your neck rope pretty high up towards the throat latch where it is about five inches from it and tighten it so it won't slide down on your horse's neck, but not tight enough to choke him. Then turn a calf out into the arena. I would still close the gates on the first few calves I roped solid. It might avoid a wreck for you, such as a calf getting into the roping box or receiving pen when you are tied hard and fast to your horn. You will have a little more rope to work with now because by using the neck rope it won't take as much rope to go through it as it did down through the chain and then back to your rein hand. So you might try two small coils in your rein hand instead of the one coil used before. Follow this calf and again pick the slowest, gentlest calf you have for this first venture. Don't carry a piggin string. At this time we are not going to tie this calf. Start out after this slow calf. Get in behind him. When everything is right, rope him. If you miss him, just stop your horse. Let the rein go if the horse will stand, and coil up your rope. Build another loop and let's say this time you catch him. Now after having roped this one (the first one the horse has roped solid) just stop him and stay on him. Let this horse watch this calf at the end of the rope. If he's taking everything steady, step down. Get a hold of the rope in front of the horse. Let it run through your hand. Go to the calf. While holding the calf around the neck with one arm, run your other hand underneath the loop. Pull the calf towards the horse. Turn the calf loose, but don't drop the rope. Start coiling it up hand over hand going to your horse. Hang it on the horn. Pat the horse. Set on him awhile. Fool with your rope, but don't pick up your rein. You want to teach this horse as long as you are not holding the rein up, you are not going to do anything. It will come in handy later when somebody comes over to untie your calf and your horse will stand quietly until asked to move ahead. All these little things seem unimportant, but we are trying to head towards one of those top kind of horses, not the lower or middle-class horse.

Now let's hope while all this is going on, you have been with somebody and learned how to tie a calf, not with any show of speed, but at least to know how to leg down a calf. The first few times you tie calves on this new green rope horse I advise legging the calves down. Mainly if things go wrong, you have a better chance of helping and watching your horse than from the flanking side. It is also easier for a green roper. After your horse is further along in his schooling, you can always go under the rope in front of your horse and start flanking the calves. But for the present where time is not important, I would leg the calves down. I would for sure not get off on the right side of this horse.

Our next step on this horse is to give him some work in the box. This particular part of his schooling has got to be done right. I've never liked the combination steer and calf chute to school a young horse on. I also like the cracks big enough in the holding pen behind the chute, and also cracks in the calf chute big enough so that the rope horse can watch the cattle in that pen and get an idea what is going on . The crack in the calf chute should not be big enough where a calf can get a leg hung up, but just be wide enough where the horse can see the hair of the calf move in the chute. I also would rather have the door of the chute swing away from the horse, so that the calf is immediately visible to the horse the split second it is released. I also like a stop behind the gate that will force the calf to come out a little to the right into the line of travel my green horse will make when he starts. I like to have the gate act as a wing to make a calf clear the width of the door. This gives the horse a chance to see the calf quicker and along with the cracks in the side of the chute lets him see the hair move in the chute, and the horse can determine when the calf is really leaving and not hanging up there as some calves will do. So much for that.

I think I forgot to mention that back cinch. It should be the wide roper's cinch and should, of course, be attached to the front one. It should also be adjusted where it rests against the hair of the horse. You adjust it this way for roping. While riding I like about one finger between the rear cinch and the hide of the horse.

You are going to have to have a helper at this stage of the horse's training and should have from this point on. Up to now you could have done everything by yourself had you chosen to do so. But loading these calves and turning them out, plus somebody to untie calves while you handle and teach your horse would be advisable. There are ways to fix an overhead rope on pulleys, so that a roper can release a calf while being in position in the box. But there is a handicap here. It doesn't take the horse long to know when you reach for the release rope, he knows the chute is going to open. He starts to watch you instead of keeping his mind on the calf in the chute. I have tried them, but I didn't like them. So I would advise against using one.

We will start this operation again without carrying a rope. We will also open our receiving pen gate down at the other end of the arena. We put on our skid boots to run these calves down to the other end. Go into this box along the far wall or fence opposite the chute. Turn your horse facing out. Then ride him up to the mouth of the empty chute. Have your helper flip the gate open while your horse is there watching. If he is jumpy about the noise the gate makes, keep him in and around the gate until he is used to the noise and until he knows it won't hurt him.

If your horse has a good light reverse or back up on him and is the type of horse we have trained throughout this book, he already has it on him. So getting back in the right-hand corner of the box shouldn't be a problem. But if he does not have such a reverse, it should be worked on prior to this box work. I would school him on his reverse out of the box.

Now there are two different ways a roping horse or dogging horse comes out of the box. One way he's backed up against the rear of the box and held on a fairly tight rein. He is released when the rider wants him to go. This horse is cocked back in a corner and when he leaves the box, he raises up in front to get out. This causes a roping horse to cover for a split second the roper's view of a calf, although the horse probably gets away just as fast as the other way. The roper is at a disadvantage as he tries to put his weight forward on this horse to help him out of the box. He is also handicapped to an extent to get with the horse's movements and causes him to take a little more time to get his rope in action. In roping every second counts when you are roping for money, so anything that hinders a roper, even though a small hindrance, is enough to cost him in tough competition.

The other way a horse leaves the box, and is the desired way, is for the horse to be not forced back against the rear of the roping box, but be about two feet from the rear in the right-hand corner. The horse should be taught to stand in this position on a rein that is not tight enough to cock his head too high but just enough restraint on those reins to hold him in there. Then this horse is capable of pulling out in front with his head lowered. The horse should also be taught never to leave until the roper pushes ahead on the rein and touches him with his legs to move out. However this horse is schooled in the beginning becomes a pattern that will probably stay with him throughout his roping career.

Now let's say our horse is ready. We have breast collar and tie-down on and we are ready to run some calves. We won't carry a rope at this time. What we will be doing is teaching the horse box manners. This is not an easy task. We want him to start out of this box when we ask him to but not break out until we signal him to start. Now have your helper load a calf, a slow one if you have one. Position your horse and give the chute help the nod for a calf. Let this calf run on out there, then take after him at a slow lope. When you leave the box get in behind the calf and run him down to the receiving pen gate. While you are chasing this calf, keep your horse in a position as much as you can at all times where you think you could rope the calf. Concentrate on this. Track about all of the five calves across the arena to your receiving pen. Say you had five head. By the time your horse is on the third or fourth calf, he will be starting to wake up and want to run a calf as soon as he hears the gate open. Repen your calves. Only this time we won't run the first two calves. We will keep the horse as quiet as we can and don't chase them. Then walk out of your box and go put the calves in the receiving pen. Don't run them. Just go in behind them and pen them. Close the gate on the pen. On this next time run a calf on across the arena to the receiving pen. Keep in behind this one. Bring him on around the pen. At the same time put your horse in the roping position. Then quit for that day. The following day come in the arena carrying a rope with your breakaway honda. Run your first calf and try to rope him. After you catch or miss, put a stop on your horse right after you have thrown. Get down and make him work a rope. Coil up and go to him. Hang the rope on the horn. Mount up and sit there for a minute with your rein down. Take your rope and make another loop. Tuck it under your arm and go back in the box. Position your horse. Nod for a calf, but don't run him. Turn out another and don't run this one either.

In scoring calves the importance of teaching this horse to stay put in the box quietly can't be emphasized enough. It is the making of a good rope horse. I would run three head of calves and score two. Let's give a few pointers on why ropers tuck a loop under their arm. This is to keep this loop high enough so it does not get hung up on your boot when you first start to swing a loop. The first movement to get your loop in action should be over and by the head of the horse and your own head. After one circle of this loop, you should concentrate on a steadying off with wrist and arm prior to a throw. The hand of the arm that has the loop tucked under it will grasp the fork of the saddle, not so that the roper can hang on, but it is used to enable the roper to help his horse to get out of the box. The split second the roper releases and signals his horse to start, he pulls himself ahead and up to get into position to rope. By the time the horse clears the box, the roper is in position by the use of this hand on the horn to start swinging a loop. He is waiting for the horse to get into position so that the roper gets a shot at the calf. These things have to be repeated so many times and coordinated to the point that it is automatic. So it will take you several hundred runs before you start to get good at it.

Let's get into this box work a little more. Let me create an illustration. If your horse is getting pretty shook up every time he's positioned waiting for a calf to be released and wants to run and face the opposite way in the corner of the box or starts to give us any other problems, take your rope off so you can work both hands. Then with a rein in each hand, go back into the box. If the horse does not want to face out, wheel this horse first in one direction a couple of complete turns, then turn him in the opposite direction a few circles. Then when he has faced out, don't turn out a calf or if you do score the calf, don't run him. Repeat this several times. Each time walk him out of the box. Go back in and give him a chance to stand straight and face out. If he repeats his former little stunt, do the same thing over.

Most horses that have speed seldom turn out to be sour box horses. It's usually the horses that lack speed and are spurred and whipped to get them close enough to rope fast calves. Then every once in awhile there's a calf with exceptionally fast speed that even crowds the fast horse to get to. Eliminate these kind of calves from the green rope horse. He will take some time to develop the split-second getaway that it takes to run these kind of calves. The calves should be slow enough that they encourage the horse and not discourage him.

If your horse is not working a good enough rope, try turning a calf loose. Before doing so, pull the calf towards the horse until you have some slack. Then get after the horse with the slack and slap him with it. Then turn the calf loose and don't tie him. Once you leave a horse and you have a calf in a loop, he figures you can't hurt him. This is why you see ropers wearing the jerk line entwined in their belt. I never liked them. I want a horse that is honest enough and wants to help me enough that he will work that rope without a jerk line. If you turn a calf loose every once in awhile instead of tying the calf, the horse is never quite sure and can't tell whether you are going to tie the calf or not. I want a horse to keep backing until the calf is down. Then all I want him to do is hold a rope just tight enough to not choke a calf, but keep just the right tension on the rope. I also like a horse that when he sees me in a flanking position, gives a little extra pull on that rope. This will help put a tough calf down. I've only owned one horse that would do this consistently. He took it on himself to do it. I don't ever remember teaching it to him. He wanted to help me put the calf down and get him tied.

Let's put in a bit here about spurs. Unless you are used to them, I would wear one spur on the left boot. If you are not used to roping, you will be hooking your right spur in your rear flank girth getting down. Once you have roped enough and worn spurs enough it won't happen but at first use just the left spur.

When the first calves are tied on a green horse, I'd rope them and then have a helper go down the rope to tie them. He should go down the rope from in front of the horse to the calf. Then he should throw and tie the calf. You can back the horse up and stop him just right as the calf is thrown and tied. You want the rope tight, but once the calf is tied, the rope should not be so tight that it chokes the calf, causing him to struggle and kick loose from the tie, when a roper is going back to his horse after completing his tie. If the horse overworks the rope at this time, it will cause the calf to struggle from having been choked and before the roper can mount up and step his horse ahead, the calf has struggled enough to get loose, causing a no-time for the roper. Another thing might be added here. Never threaten or get after your horse when going to him after tying the calf. You want to go to your horse after tying your calf in a deliberate slow pace. Do not raise your arms or run to him. If you are roping five calves a day and score three or four, this is enough in the young horse's training. If he is overworking a rope, say "Whoa" at him every time he does it. He will get the idea when to stop. If he doesn't, put him on a big calf or two. This will cause him to slow down. If he doesn't work a rope enough, rope a light one. Run to the calf. Pull him towards the horse throwing the slack at the horse. Then as we said before, turn the calf loose.

I've tried to cover the training of this rope horse. If he has even half the previous training done right on him from the time he was started up to the time we started him at reining, he will turn out to be a rope horse. If he has had the full course of training I have described in this book, and a good roper that knows his business gets him to train, there is no reason why this horse should not go to the top, providing he has the speed. I think I'll finish these instructions on the rope horse by saying that lap and tap ropers foul up more good horses by starting too soon and trying to meet the calf at the gate than where your horse can see him before you start. Don't be waiting at the gate to meet the calf. This gets a horse over anxious in the box quicker than any other thing.

We covered the reining horse stop in our writing on the reining horses. We also gave the contrast of the two ways it was done as the two different types of events required each horse to do. I'll go further on this rope horse stop to clarify and guide you more on the subject. The stop on the rope horse should be implemented on him prior to roping. This is how it is done.

If the horse does not have any experience in stopping, do the following: With your roping rein in your right hand, put your horse in a slow lope in a straight line. Say "whoa" sharp and clear. Then place your left hand on your horse's neck about a foot from his ears. The thumb will be on the right side of his neck. The four fingers of your hand will be on the left side. Put your hand on his neck and bear down. Wait one or two seconds. Then come back on your reins. When you come back on them, feel for contact with his mouth lightly. Then when you feel you have connected with it, increase your pressure. Do not remove your hand from the horse's neck until the stop is completed. One other thing that goes with these two actions is raise up and off the rear quarters of your horse before you apply either the neck touch or the rein pressure. As soon as the horse completes the stop, release your rein pressure. Repeat this stop at a slow lope using the described methods several times. Then eliminate the command "whoa." Then try just the neck stop using your reins in your left hand and using the same hand to touch his neck. The last measure is used so that you can use it when actually roping to further and improve his stop. I have gone to the hackamore bit for this purpose on some horses to acquaint him with the stop and to save his mouth. Once he's responding to the neck stop, he can then be put back in the bit. Once you have thrown the rope at a calf, your right hand, after pitching the slack away from the horse so he does not get over the rope with his front feet and thus giving him room to stop, goes direct to the saddle horn preparing to dismount. Your left hand, now free from the coil of rope, can then be placed on the horse's neck. The last move made is to come back on the reins for the stop.

In winding this subject up, one thing I failed to mention is relax when working a green horse at anything you are trying to teach him. This is a hard thing to do. Even experienced trainers have difficulty at it. But practice it. It will pay dividends, especially in the roping box. Horses have an instinct in their capacity to know when you are over tense. They do react to it. Get and stay ready, but control it. The horse will know it.

 **23**

The Rearing Horse

Throughout my training career I've taken about every kind of spoiled horse I think there is. These horses for the most part were started by inexperienced people that probably made a lot of mistakes in the handling of them. Because I was not financially able to turn them down, I took them. My only regret is that I should have charged more for these kinds of horses than I did the good horses I schooled because the risk was greater. I never did. After I had ridden a couple of hundred horses, all breeds entered the picture. In the past seven years I was in the training business, I received better stock. Seventy-five percent of them were registered quarter horses. The others were a "duke's mixture" of Arabs, half Arabs, half quarter horse, and some just plain horses. I started quite a few thoroughbreds that were two to three years old for the track. My earlier training consisted of bronc or bronc-type horses. These horses advanced my knowledge of horses as far as being able to ride them was concerned. After many sessions with the broncs, the other horses, even though spoiled, didn't seem all that bad to me. However, some of these rearing up horses, if chronic, were dangerous. They were for the most part fairly gentle horses other than this rearing up habit.

Let us break these horses down a bit into a few different categories. Let's take the two-year-old first. These horses as a rule have not reached the stage where they are chronic. They have a habit of being what I call a little light on the front end. Then there's the older type that's maybe a four or five-year-old or even older, that some horseman who wanted to look like an old-time movie star, and thought he was really doing some thing great to get and encourage a horse to rear up. This type horse would do it on the least provocation on a pull of the bit, but didn't come all the way over. The dangerous-type horse in these rearing up animals are the ones that mean business. They come all the way over. If you don't have a way of counteracting this habit, they will hurt you. The methods we are going to describe will cure most of them and straighten them out.

In most young horses the cause was the use of curb bits on tender mouths too soon, before they had a chance to be schooled. They found out that by rearing up, they could scare the person riding them into getting off. When they came up pretty high, the rider would dismount. If a horse accomplishes this about three times in a row, he knows the score and has gotten this through his head. This little move he makes will eliminate the agony or aggravation on his back for the moment.

To cure these rearing horses, I'm sure you have heard of the following techniques: There's the one about the two-by-four taken with the rider when he mounts up. When the critter comes up in front, he lets him have it right between the ears, knocking him unconscious and all the way to the ground. Then this rider told me when the horse regained his senses, he mounted again carrying the two-by-four and from that day on the horse never repeated the rearing up tactic. However, I was always afraid of killing somebody's horse. Although I've never had occasion to see this put into action, I really couldn't call the guy a liar. But rest assured, I was somewhat skeptical.

Then there was the paper bag filled with water method. This I tried by having my wife fill up several paper bags of water. Each time the horse started to rear, I would try to bust the paper bag of water on his head. Most of the time it busted before I could bust the horse with it. After several sacks, I'd be soaking wet and what water didn't splash on me when the sack would break before I could land it on the dome of the horse while he was standing pretty much straight up on his hind legs. I would be leaning forward almost on his ears to keep him down. I decided there must be a better way.

Now let's get down to something that makes a little more sense. I found most of these horses did not want to or wouldn't turn one way or the other or didn't want to rein, period. I found that when reined to right or left, whichever way he did not like to go, he would rear, or the least pull on the bit to make him back would also induce it. Some were cold backed. If you cinched them tight enough to hold a saddle, when you mounted they would flip over and I mean just flat throw themselves. I would say over a fifteen-year period, I received at least twenty of these horses of different breeds that were all in the same bag. They reared up. Some were bad, some mediocre, and some that didn't give me too much trouble. Some of them were responsible for people being crippled and are still crippled today, before I got them. Some of them are dangerous and should not be monkeyed with by inexperienced people. Even some trainers don't really know how to cure one.

What sort of got me on the right track to figure out a way to keep these horses out of this habit was the fact that I had never started a horse that ever got the habit. I figured the best way was to start him all over again. I also knew I was going to run into more obstacles by applying the same methods I used on young colts. So I figured I'd have to use more pressure on them knowing for the most part they were bad-mouthed horses. I would start the horse back in a fiador hackamore. I had an old bosal with a steel cable running through it and plaited rawhide wrapped that was strictly for hard-headed old bronc horses. I'd put this hackamore on this rearing up horse. I would tie his head around to the left by running one rein under and around the latigo. The first time I didn't tie him too short, just enough where he would bend his head just a little in that direction. I had a good breaking pen with the corners rounded off. Then I got after this horse with a lunge line on him and a lunging whip. After a few circles, instead of giving me his head to the right even though he was tied short enough to induce him to do so, he just lowered his head to his chest. Although he would make the circle, he would not turn his head. So I stopped him and took off my lunge line. This time I shortened up the rein tied to the latigo about another foot. Standing about in the position where you would cinch the horse up, I would take and bring his head around where his nose almost touched my left elbow. I tied the rein off real easy so as not to spook him and stepped back away from him. He stood with his neck arched trying to straighten it out by lowering his head. But he couldn't make it. Finally he started giving that rein a little slack. After turning several times on his own, he tried to rear with the empty saddle. But that didn't work either. He then managed to throw himself in the process. He got up and I started to force him to turn by getting just behind his head and neck. Every time he turned I'd repeat getting in position to make him turn again. It wasn't long before he was turning freely when I'd get after him. I left him in that position for about twenty minutes. Then I tied his head the other way to the billet on the right side. I did this every day for a week. I would then lunge this horse after every one of these sessions with his head free. I did not ride him at all the first week.

At the beginning of the second week, I took this horse out of the breaking pen. I put a lunge line on the end of the two hackamore reins. I stood about fifteen feet away from the fence or wall. I told my helper to run this horse between me and the fence. He was not on the horse. The saddle was empty. When this horse got to about a forty-five-degree angle from and ahead of me I hollered "whoa" at him. Then I set down on my line When he hit it, he swapped ends. He stood there and looked at me. I went up to him and patted him. I again had my helper break him into a gallop from the opposite direction. I hollered "whoa" at him and set down on the line. He hit the end of reins and line just about as hard as the first time. The third time he went into a gallop by me. When I hollered "whoa," he gathered up and was bending to the right on the hackamore reins and the line before he hit it. Now this doubling back of a horse in the hackamore is not the nicest way to treat a horse. In this case where the horse was a chronic rearing up horse, I figured it would call for some extreme measures. We went back to the breaking pen and lunged this horse. Then I put him away. On the tenth day I mounted him with the hackamore on him. He gave his head to me with a side pull immediately. I rode him around at a walk. I finally broke into a trot. I had my helper stand in the middle of the pen with the lunging whip. He turned with the horse as though he were lunging the horse. I gave the horse a command "whoa" and pulled lightly on the reins. He stopped. I patted him and talked soothingly to him and pulled or started to pull him in the opposite direction. But just as he had turned, he stopped and started to come up in front. I was carrying a bat, and I came down as hard as I could between his ears with it. I then spurred him forward. He started shaking his head and went on. It was the one and only time that he ever tried it with me. This same horse had come over backwards and put his owner in the hospital for the summer before he came to me. He was sold out of my stable, and I saw young girls riding him that summer.

I'll point out here that I could not have done the same thing with this horse in a bit without ruining what mouth he had left on him. I put him in a ring snaffle before he left my training stable. He turned out to be a useful saddle horse from that time on. I think the success of this venture was in making this horse know that he could be turned. Once you get one limbered up in the neck enough, you can bend him and make him go on before he has a chance to come up in front.

Let us go back over these instructions carefully. How did we change this horse? I think the introduction to the hackamore, then the absence of a bit which the horse had a dread of, was one factor. Then having tied this horse's head around in both directions forcing him to turn, and by making him realize that he could be controlled with his head down, we were starting to change his mind about rearing up. The fact that this was all done on the ground with no risk to the rider had also added to its success. This horse should also be taught to back up in the hackamore before going back to a bit. By teaching the horse a light side pull, we could use a counter measure at the instant he decided to come up in front. This caused the horse to be in a turning position which made it impossible for him to rear. Because to be successful for the horse to rear, he has to be in a straight position, so that his hind legs can support his action. By getting a good light bend on the horse, then going on with it in his actual riding, he had been disadvantaged from trying it. Had this horse been started right, the rearing up habit would have never occurred, with one exception, which is the cinch-bound, cold-backed horse. I have found the only answer in correction of this type horse is to lunge him or pony him with another horse with the cinch tightened until he is warmed up. Then as a general rule this horse can be ridden with a degree of safety and will sometimes cure him as his training progresses.

 **24**

Barrel Horse

Most horses to make good barrel horses should have some preparatory schooling before actual barrel training begins. Too many people will take a horse that is not much more than broken and has a slow neckrein on him. They will set up three barrels and put a horse on them, regardless of the horse's past schooling. They seem to think that all you have to do is start loping around those barrels day after day and that the horse will make a good barrel horse.

My idea differs from this. I've trained a few and watched a lot of them. I'm firmly convinced, if done right, a horse should have a lot of extensive training away from the barrels before he even looks at them. A rope horse can go into a box and stand quietly and then start in a split second going wide open after a calf. Once the calf is roped and tied, he remains quiet while the roper remounts. He then will go back in the box and does the same thing all over again without blowing up or generally acting a little nutty. Then why not the barrel horse? A barrel horse should be able to start and in two jumps be wide open, then after making a run should stop after crossing the finish line. He should be able to walk out of that arena without too much reaction after the run.

Let's explore the reasons why there are so many uncontrolled barrel horses. One of the factors involved is the riders have to make sure that the horse is in the proper lead to go to right or left on the first barrel. The rider makes one or two little circles to the right or left according to which barrel they are taking first, or they offset the horse to accomplish this. At this time the horse has been turned away from the barrel, then all of a sudden turned back towards the first barrel. He has been confused by not having time to look in the direction of the first barrel. When he has been wheeled to the right and jumped out, he just gets a glimpse of the barrel and he is there. Now let's take a well-reined horse that you can start on either lead when cued and do it from a split-second start into wide open speed. You could take this horse out a few yards in front of the starting line and let him settle and look at that first barrel and go. Which horse do you think would do the best job getting around that first barrel? I think the honest answer would be the last type of horse that had had a chance to look and study where he's headed.

Now let us take a look at the young horse that is put on barrels that hasn't had some reining training. He is broke and has a slow rein on him but does not have a flying change of leads behind. After repeatedly running to that second barrel and he has had to change hind leads on the second barrel to make a turn he finds it awkward and does not change behind. He cannot make a united turn on the barrel. If he is repeatedly run at this second barrel and does not change hind leads from the first to the second barrel, he starts to make a big turn on this barrel or hates to try to make the turn because he is in the wrong lead. He then gets the rider mad. The rider makes up his mind that the horse is going to turn that barrel whether he thinks he can or not. So he takes the bat and shortens up his inside rein and pours the leather to the horse's neck. The horse now concentrates not on his mistake of not changing leads behind, but on the pain that is taking place on his mouth and neck. The horse is shook up, and he is already starting to hate those barrels. Then when he is coming home to the finish line, no matter how hard he runs, and in most cases he's giving everything he has got, he gets whipped and spurred for more speed. He soon gets the idea that all those barrels hold for him is misery. Again he hates the barrels more. It isn't long before we aren't really riding a controlled horse anymore. We cannot pinpoint in our reining of him to help him if he hasn't had reining training. All we have is a half-controlled runaway horse with probably very little mouth left, if any.

Now suppose we have put three months' training on the horse. That is the kind of training written about in the fore part of this book, and we can change the hind leads on the horse when we cue him. We can do a three hundred sixty degree turn on him. He is also used to pivoting on either hind foot. We take the same pains to let him look at those barrels as we would with the rope horse. Sometimes we would make a run at those barrels and sometimes we would just set and score the barrlels. This means that we would spend a lot of time sitting facing the barrel that we were to run at first in a relaxed manner. Then we woud not start the run, but just ride off in another direction. When we do make a run, this horse with enough training should be able to start in the desired lead from a walk to go to the first barrel. If he has the right kind of reining training on him, we could then pinpoint him to the exact distance from the barrel to make the turn. Now let us assume that we are using the right-hand barrel. The horse starts in his right hind lead as he makes the turn and is now heading for the second barrel. At some point between the first and second barrel, the horse has to make a flying change of leads from right hind lead to left hind lead. This is the point that confuses the horse the most. If he has been taught a change of leads behind, this is easy for him to accomplish and allows him to make a smooth turn around the second barrel. As the horse approaches the last barrel, he will stay in his left lead until finishing the run.

In contrast between the horse that has had the reining training, plus having perfected the flying change of leads behind, running the barrels is made easy for him. Whereas the other horse that has to be taught these things while in the process of running barrels has a lot of strikes against him going in. A few horses make it, but a lot of them start to figure out ways to get out of these impossible situations as this is the way he starts to view them.

Here's the way it should go with the trained horse. We can start in the correct lead. Then our horse is well reined enough where we can take dead aim about two feet to the left of that first barrel, then bend him around our right leg and jump him out towards that second barrel. Cue for a left change of leads behind. Aim at the second barrel. Then wind him around our left leg staying in the left lead. On a light-reined horse, you can check him a little going into the turn on the third barrel. Then ask him to run his best and not overuse the bat and spurs on the home stretch. When we have crossed that finish line, give the horse a prior signal using the neck stop. Let him settle a few seconds and ride off at a walk. I believe roper's skid boots should be used on these barrel horses.

Most of the good barrel horses that are consistent are horses that have had a lot of basic training. They have to have speed going in. These horses in their early training have had good hands schooling them, and most of them show good results and good runs. The horses that are put on barrels without it never get to the top, not always, but average out losers because they are not and cannot be controlled horses. They have to have skill and maneuverability. Only good training can accomplish this and keep a good mouth on the horse. The more you have to beat and spur a young horse in his early barrel training stages, the harder it is for him to think. I think they can be overtrained in making too many practice runs.

The rate of speed from first to second barrel has to be pretty fast so that the horse that is not schooled on a change of leads behind can be offset to the right and booted with the right leg and spur to change that lead behind. I'm talking about bringing the horse's head to the right and putting pressure on his right side with leg and spur for a left lead change. I think you should lengthen out those two barrels to give you more time to accomplish this. Start to push him into that lead some distance from the second barrel to make sure he is in his left lead to make the turn. I also think that trotting around the barrels and even walking around them are okay. But slow loping around them is a mistake. I don't think practice runs should be made at a lope, but about medium speed. I don't think you should open up coming home only occasionally. I would, however, ask him to run wide open once in awhile. I would also not start my horse wide open coming into an arena gate, nor would I run him out the gate that they are doing so much of now at horse shows and many rodeos. Once in awhile it is necessary, but most of the time it is not. A little more thought on this if given by horse show committees and rodeo committees would go a long ways to stop making runaways out of barrel horses. If you barrel riders would go in a group at a show and ask the committee in a nice way to change this part of it, I believe they would and could.

I believe in a rein in each hand and a tiedown on a barrel horse in the early stages of his training. I also believe if he has had enough reining training prior to putting him on barrels, he will come out a better and more consistent winning horse. So you people who are shopping for a barrel horse to start might keep in mind that an ex-reining horse might have some merit, if he has speed and isn't fouled up and is sound.

In conclusion of this writing on the barrel horse, I would advise people buying one or starting a new barrel horse that half of this horse's pedigree should have some race breeding in it, such as Leo, Three Bars, or other racing bloodlines. You can train a horse to a razor's edge, but if he doesn't have enough speed to compete in a speed event, he'll get outrun by horses that have it.

25

Trailer Schooling

In beginning these discussions of horse trailers and the following instructions on how to load horses in them, it might be helpful to talk about types of trailers. The single horse trailer is probably the hardest type trailer to teach a horse to load into. The easiest type is the so-called combination stock horse and cattle trailer that is made with the cracks between the slats. It would be for four horses or more. Horses do not seem to fear this kind of trailer. It's a great advantage for moving loose mares and foals or yearlings. I think the fact that they can see daylight on the sides and perhaps the larger area has a lot to do with it. Most of the time horses can be driven into this type trailer from a small pen or stall. They don't seem to mind too much to be led into them either. But most horses are moved and hauled in the two-horse models of the different makes. There are many ways people accomplish loading horses. Some by coaxing, some by baiting with feed or tidbits. I am not at odds with their methods. I have loaded green horses in large numbers into a lot of different makes of trailers. After trying different methods, I condensed it down to one method that was as nearly foolproof and timesaving as I could. I found that I had to take every advantage of the horse that I could. I also had to figure out all the angles to keep from injuring them.

A lot of horses are injured and spoiled by people using wrong methods while teaching them to load. When a trailer hooked to any vehicle is standing in the open and you are in the process of trying to load a greenie, the horse if he doesn't want to load, and most of them don't, has a lot of advantage, regardless of how much help you have. If you are alone or only have one person to help you, the situation can almost be impossible loading a stubborn spoiled horse. So I will try to show you a way that should work for you in the following writing, whether your trailer is a single or a two-horse trailer.

This is the way to start. Back this trailer up to the side of a building or the corner of one. Put it in a position along a wall or a side of a pen where you can use the wall or the side of a pen like a wing. Now you can be at a little angle with your trailer to the wall, but the angle can't be so much that the horse going into the trailer using the wall or pen as a buffer or wing is at too much of an angle. The horse will be suspicious of the curve. So the straighter the angle the better. Most horse trailers have two small openings in front of either side of the trailer with little doors on them. These are made so the people or handlers can reach in and unsnap the horse prior to unloading or to secure the horse after loading. On each side of the manger is a tie ring made of steel. You should have a sturdy snap and short length of tie rope already attached to these rings. So once the horse is in the trailer and the door is closed at the rear after the butt chain is fastened, you can reach in this little door and snap the stationary snap on to the horse's halter and unsnap the lead rope used to guide the horse in. Some trailers have a side or escape door on one side or the other. Some have two escape doors on them. These present less trouble to load a horse than do the ones we first mentioned with just the two little window-type doors. Regardless, more or less the same procedures to load won't be too much different.

With our trailer backed up to the side of a building or the side of a high pen, we will now need as part of our equipment a long piece of rope. A good strong lunge line with a strong snap is all right. Any piece of nylon rope twenty-five feet long with a strong snap is okay. You may also use a limp old calf rope, but make sure you use a heavy snap on it. It takes two people to operate this method. The half door or one single door of the trailer at the rear will be against the fence wall or gate that we are using as a wing or buffer on one side of the horse. The wall or fence should be high enough where the horse cannot get his head over it, because under pressure if a fence is used, he might try to jump over it. What happens when you try to load one in the open is he will stick his head over the door of the trailer and try to go around that way. Then he will try to go around the other. The longer he does this, the more he will try not to go in. So let's get mister horse out and put this twenty-five foot piece of rope on him. Make sure your halter is adjusted to where he won't pull it off up over his nose. It should be a pretty stout halter.

Now we have this trailer door open, and it must remain open. This open door should be secured to the wall or fence if possible to make sure at just about the time the horse decides he's going to load, his movements or the wind doesn't make it swing shut, hitting the horse's side and hinder him from wanting to go in. The other door of the trailer should be closed, as he's sure to stick his head in there if it's open. He will try everything except that which we want him to do, go in the door on the side we want him to. Your colt or horse can be real good halter broke, but when asked to lead into a trailer for the first few times will rebel and balk at going in. So we now give this long rope to our helper standing in front of the trailer by the hitch at one of these little doors. He takes the rope. Then we give him the following instructions. We will instruct him that this horse is going to look into the trailer at some point and maybe step in with both front feet, hesitate, then back out. Let him do so. We will also tell him to make sure he does not get a rap around his hand with this long rope, nor shall he get the long end or slack wrapped around the hitch or any part of the tow vehicle. Tell him to keep the rope to one side of the trailer in the clear, so he does not get caught in it if the horse decides to come back out fast. Then the last and one of the main things we instruct him to do is just keep the horse's head in line with the entrance to the trailer and take up slack if the horse starts to enter. But give him slack if he wants to back out. Once we have the colt in, we gently close and lock the door on him. The helper should proceed using a steady (not jumpy) hand to snap the tie snap on the horse, but not until he gets the signal from the rear man that the door is closed.

We are now ready for the rear man's instructions. Place a little grain in the feed manger at the front of the trailer, then about half-way up on the trailer floor towards the front end, sprinkle some on the floor. Have a short whip in your hand. What we are going to teach this horse is that he wants to go in that hole that is the trailer door. The operator from the rear gives the front man instructions when to pull to straighten the horse's head to keep it in line with the trailer entrance, as the front man's vision may be obscured at times by the small window he's watching the horse through. Now step behind the horse and urge him forward. Your position should be at an angle, partially behind and partially to the side, so you can discourage him from going sideways or back. As the horse approaches the trailer entrance, let him stand and at this point give this horse all the time he needs to inspect the entrance to the trailer and smell of it. Then have the front man or helper take his free hand and shake a little grain in the manger, making sure the horse can see it. After the horse has inspected and smelled the inside of the trailer, start to urge him forward. He'll hesitate, but keep urging him, putting on a little more pressure. Don't whip the horse. Just touch him a little on his rump or lightly on his back legs. He will finally start in. But only put two front feet in. He will hesitate and come back out and maybe two lengths of his body back. Don't worry. Just get in behind him. He will either load on this attempt or the third attempt after he has backed out. He has gone into the trailer in the first instance to inspect it further and did not really mean to go all the way in, but he will go in after a few tries.

Sometimes a horse will get in, but will still have two hind feet out right next to the edge of the trailer. Tell your helper even though he's stretched out and could be tied off in front, not to tie until both hind feet are in the trailer. If he's tied off at this point, you could easily break his leg, if he decided to back out. Touch a hind leg lightly with the whip and keep touching first one, then the other. He will put in one leg and finally the other leg. Then quietly close your door. Hook your butt chain and tell the helper to tie him off. Once a horse is loaded in this manner about three times, he will go in the trailer in the open using the same methods.

We have now described how to load the horse, but we have not told you how to unload him. It works both ways on some horses. After they load, they won't unload. Now if you only have one horse in a two-horse trailer, it is quite easy to go on the opposite side of the empty entrance. If the horse refuses to back out, take your long rope that you used to load him with and another lead rope. Attach one to each side of his halter ring at the bottom. Run them out behind the horse, one on each side like a pair of driving reins. Then standing behind him, pull him back. Keep the slack out of your lines. Hold him solid and keep pulling. He will finally back out.

If it is a side escape door trailer, have your helper stand there and push back on the horse. This is one way to get him out without getting in between him and the manger and run the risk of his crushing you.

I forgot to mention one of the main reasons we don't pull on this horse to get him to load into the trailer is the fact that if you try to hold him in once he is half in, and he decides to pull back, the first thing he will do is raise his head and hit the top of the trailer. Once he does this about twice, he'll make up his mind that there is something in the trailer that's going to hurt him. It has the same reaction that a horse has when he's been beaten over the head and ears by some person.

When you are teaching this horse to load, let him set in the trailer for ten minutes eating a little grain. Then go down the road a short ways. Come back and unload him. Then reset your trailer as before and load him again and unload him. Make sure he is latched and has stood for a few minutes before repeating. In applying this method of loading the horse and in conclusion of this article, let me say that if you follow the instructions written here, you will accomplish the job. Use patience.

There is one other method that I have used that has worked for me successfully. If you are in a position that requires you to attempt to load a horse by yourself, put your trailer in the same position as mentioned in the previous method. Then go into your trailer with the long rope attached to your horse. Run this end of the long rope through the tie ring. Then come back out of the trailer with all the slack in your hand. Get to the side and rear of the animal. Then with the slack of your rope in your left hand and short whip in your right hand, follow the same procedures explained in the two-man operation. The success of this operation is letting the horse investigate every part of the trailer before urging him forward. Once the horse is loaded, gently close your door. Fasten your butt chain. Take a wrap around the center support of your trailer. Snap your stationary snap onto the horse's halter and unsnap your long lead rope. Then go to the rear of the trailer and coil up your long rope. This method will work for you most of the time, but is not as good as the two-man operation.

You will finally have convinced the horse to want to load and that he didn't get hurt in the process. He soon learns not to fear the trailer. Try it. It works.

One last addition. The person operating from the rear of this horse would perhaps do well to use voice communication with the horse. When he is progressing favorably to load, use the words, "Good boy, good boy," soothingly. When he is rebelling, scold him sharply. Your voice will help make the difference here.

Conclusion

In winding up this book I'll say that the methods and procedures were tried, tested, and I found they worked if time and patience were adhered to. Horses are like people to an extent, in many respects. Each one has its own little traits, mostly good, but in some instances a little bad. If given enough direction at the right age, they turn out well. There are problem people. There will also always be problem horses. Most problem horses, if corrected in time using the right methods, can be straightened out. There will always be a few, that for whatever reason they have, never really submit completely in their acceptance of people. They are in the minority. Most spoiled horses are not born that way. They get that way from wrong handling.

To me horses have always been a part of my life. I think they have contributed a lot of good to my life also. To me they aren't just an animal. I'm aware they have their hurts and joys, too. They are proud, tough and intelligent, and they have contributed so much to man. They will never get the recognition due them. My hope was that if I could make a useful horse out of the animal through training, he would perhaps be thought enough of for his ability that he would have a better home and be fed, sheltered and cared for, especially in the winter months. Nothing bugs me more than to see these animals in a short pasture with no windbreak and fenced in where they can't find shelter from a blizzard. So, folks, think about it. If he's worth owning, he's worth taking care of.